Common Sense Truth

An Accurate Account of the Fall of the United States

By Dan Fragoules

Cover Photo by Todd Trapani

Printed in the United States of America

First Printing, 2021

ISBN: 979-8-9850477-1-4

Barren Creek Publishing
1341 Barren Creek Road
Mountain Home AR 72653

www.barrencreek.com

Contents

Forward

When I wrote my first book in 2008, I believed our country could still be saved. I spoke at Tea Party rallies, appeared on talk radio and supported candidates I believed would fight for liberty. I was wrong. The ruling class does not allow peasants to interfere with their power. The only thing left to do, is to document what happened while it can still be written.

"When the first atomic bomb was exploded in New Mexico, the desert sand turned to fused green glass. Archaeologists digging in the ancient Euphrates Valley have uncovered a layer of agrarian culture 8,000 years old, a layer of herdsmen culture much older, and a still older caveman culture. Recently they reached another layer, a layer of fused green glass."

New York Herald Tribune, 1947

Conspiracy Theory

The term "conspiracy theory" was coined by supporters of the Warren Commission to discredit those who doubted the finding that Lee Oswald acted alone to kill President Kennedy. From that moment, the definition of "conspiracy theory" was no longer an event explained by a conspiracy, it's anything that questions the official explanation.

By 1963 the people who ordered Kennedy's execution and forced the official explanation for it on a public that clearly had doubts, had been running this country for fifty years. They are still in power. They were not elected, they control who gets elected. They control the distribution of information and they systematically discredit anyone who questions their version of events which are always calculated to obscure the connections between succeeding events that would expose their agenda.

Many "conspiracy theories" that we haven't given credence to, that we have been actively discouraged from taking seriously, look altogether different when viewed in the context of their relation to previous events. The truth behind the official explanations reveals a continuity to event after supposedly random event in which those explanations consistently fail to agree with the evidence, and consistently benefit the same small group of wealthy people. The pandemic, border crisis, civil unrest and election irregularities were not unrelated incidents, and they were not accidents. They are just the most recent in a pattern of offensives in a war on America as founded, on private property and individual liberty, which began over a hundred years ago.

The first attack was orchestrated by a consortium of banking dynasties who after bribing Congress for several years and slipping not a few dollars to President Taft, backed Woodrow Wilson's 1912 presidential bid. Their work culminated in 1913 with the Federal Reserve Act and ratification of the 16th Amendment. It gave them direct, permanent access to the paychecks of American workers, complete control of the money supply and it put the power of the ruling class and its bureaucracy on a self-sustaining trajectory of escalating expansion. When it crossed the line from being a servant of the people to master can be debated, that it had to cross it is inarguable.

The American people did not vote for a tax on their own wages, nor did they consent to Congress giving away its constitutional power to coin money to a private corporation owned by the world's largest banks. The Federal Reserve Act and the 16th Amendment were frauds on the American people committed by the Warburgs, Rothschilds, Morgans and Rockefellers. These were the founding members of an unelected ruling class that has controlled the government and economy of the United States ever since.

The Federal Reserve is a global entity, controlled by a handful of billionaires that from the day it was created has had complete control over how much money is available for the government to spend and how much is available to retail banks and consumers. It replaced indiscriminate market forces with a system controlled by the ruling elite. It put too much power in too few hands, and it led to the largest transfer of wealth from the masses to the elite in history. Their actions caused a Great Depression that we were told was an act of nature. It was larceny, and the untold human suffering it caused was merely collateral damage in an illegal business deal.

The income tax, Federal Reserve and Great Depression were just the beginning of a coordinated shift of money and political power from the people and their state and local governments to the federal government where it could be controlled by the ruling class whose appetite for power has only grown in the years since. Eisenhower, who recognized it as the military industrial complex, warned his successor who attempted to take steps to control it. Kennedy brokered peace deals in North Africa and Southeast Asia where covert CIA operations were working to secure oil and mineral reserves for the Morgan and Rockefeller corporations, he signed an order that stripped the Federal Reserve of its power to loan money to the government and gave the U.S. Treasury Department the authority to issue money. Three weeks later he was dead.

Kennedy's replacement, Lyndon Johnson, was a small-time organized crime boss who rigged an election to get into the Senate and likely became President by being an accessory to murder. As the ruling class's first wholly illegitimate President, Johnson presided over the next shift of power from the people to our rulers. He sent a half million

3

kids to fight an undeclared war in Southeast Asia, expanded Social Security to include Medicare and Medicaid, federalized the education system, and took the first steps toward gaining centralized control of the distribution of information.

Johnson and most of his successors serve a covertly unified governing authority who put on a show of Republican verses Democrat to divide the people into manageable teams with mascots, logos and slogans. MSNBC and CNN cheer on the blue team while Fox News and Talk Radio spur the red to outrage over superficial issues while behind the scenes, ruling class billionaires loot the country. Mass media from Saturday morning cartoons to cable news, every Google search and every social media site, propagate a prescribed narrative that we have been predisposed to accept by years of increasingly not so subtle indoctrination in government schools.

That might sound like an impossibly large and intricate conspiracy, but it is run of the mill oligarchic population control. It's how Hitler, Stalin and many others brought entire nations along with their madness. They control what the truth is, even when no one believes it. They control who might be in a position to run for national office and they control the hundreds of thousands if not millions of dollars and the blessing of sanctioned media it takes to win a national election. The only difference party makes is which half of the electorate believes they had a say. Sometimes your side wins, sometimes it loses. The only constant is that either way nothing changes.

When a candidate or twenty slip through the system it makes little difference. Power is awarded for loyalty and cooperation, not conferred by an election. A newly elected member of Congress who has sold out to no one, goes to Washington to defend the Constitution and represent her constituents, but finds that she is for all practical purposes, powerless unless she demonstrates her usefulness to the ruling establishment. The more useful she is, the more successful her career. The direct successors to the 1913 ruling class exert enormous influence over who holds positions of power in Congress, and they've had at least some control over every Presidential election since 1912.

When Joseph Kennedy used his ruling class connections to help his son get elected, he accepted Lyndon Johnson as part of the bargain. John Kennedy made the mistake of believing he was in charge. When Nixon made the same mistake, they replaced his Vice President, sent the same CIA operatives that had run the Bay of Pigs invasion to the Watergate, and Gerald Ford became the next leader of the free world

4

to have been hand-picked by the ruling class. After Ford had served his purpose, Carter was allowed to win the next election because he wasn't deemed likely to cause much trouble, especially given that they controlled interest rates and the money supply and could create whatever economic conditions they needed.

Reagan's union and acting careers gave him the contacts and experience to understand how to both use, and to articulate the danger of the ruling class. He also knew better than to challenge them and accepted the C.I.A.'s own George H.W. Bush as his Vice President. Under Bush's direction, the Department of Justice, CIA, Bill Clinton and a drug runner for the Medellín drug cartel called Barry Seal conducted secret flights out of Mena Arkansas carrying M-16 rifles to Nicaragua where they were traded for cocaine. Seal died in a gun fight in Baton Rouge, Bush and Clinton became the next two Presidents. They were followed by George W Bush, who brought his family's banking, oil and CIA connections to work with him. He was followed by a community organizer who owed his Senate seat to the same Chicago political machine that helped rig the 1960 Presidential election. After Obama, we were set up to accept Hillary with no questions asked.

That was the situation a total outsider stepped into in 2015. The ruling class in the guise of Federal law enforcement, made the determination that Trump was a threat shortly after he announced his candidacy. That threat designation justified actions that would have been overtly treasonous in a functioning Republic. The Chairman of the Joint Chiefs and directors of the FBI, CIA and NSA worked with compromised members of Congress and sanctioned media to destroy Trump's Presidency. Trump, unaware of the true nature of what lay beneath the surface of the swamp he intended to drain was unprepared for the assault on his candidacy, Presidency and family.

The FBI raided the homes and offices of Trump associates, arresting them on charges of "making contradictory statements" during questioning. The FBI worked with the DNC and the Clinton campaign to forge documents purported to be evidence of collusion between Trump and Russia. Agents instigated a plot in Michigan to kidnap the governor, then arrested their own co-conspirators and claimed that they were Trump supporters. The Chairman of the Joint Chiefs of Staff ordered officials at the Military Command Center to run any orders from the Commander in Chief by him while he prepared for a military takeover of civilian government in the event a 2020 coup failed. Undercover FBI agents at the Capital on January 6th encouraged the crowd to enter the building where the most highly funded police force in the country had prepared an ambush of Trump supporters who were upset over a third world style election.

The actual insurrectionists had just stolen an election they hadn't yet gotten away with. The "insurrection" was orchestrated to discredit efforts to expose the most serious crime against representative government in the United States since the Kennedy brother's executions. The red and blue media joined forces and the official explanation, as far as you could tell by watching Television or social media, was accepted by all. Republican and Democrat politicians put the 2020 election behind them and we the people were forbidden to so much as question their actions. "We can't look back" they say. Of course, we can't. If we look back, we might see how they all became multi-millionaires on a congressman's salary.

The National Security "threat" posed by Trump and his voters was justification for U.S. taxpayer funds to be used to pay for gain of function research in a foreign bio-weapons lab. The money, authorized by Anthony Fauci, Director of the National Institute of Allergy and Infectious Diseases, financed ongoing research into viral means of population and demographic control. Started by the CIA after WWII, the experiments were moved from American labs to Wuhan China because the Chinese government was better at keeping secrets, were largely immune from bad publicity and provided plausible deniability to U.S. officials.

As far as the ruling establishment was concerned, a virus that purportedly killed 600,000 Americans, was not a national security threat or even worthy of investigation, but an unarmed protest at the Capital where no buildings were burned, no stores were looted and no cops were attacked was cause for impeachment, hundreds of arrests, years of investigation and the full force of federal law enforcement turned against *white domestic terrorists* because the greatest threat facing the country, at least the part of it behind razor wire at the Capital, were people who believed the 2020 election was fraudulent.

Spying on U.S. citizens, paying for Chinese bio-weapon research and changing the outcome of a Presidential election would not have been possible in a free country and is a testament to how the war has progressed since its 1913 inception. "National Security" was redefined to mean defending an unelected shadow government and the system on which its power depends against a population that failed to support their designated candidate. It's the same method Kim Jong-un used to stay in control of North Korea.

As the ruling class expanded its power, corrupt politicians amassed fortunes and multinational corporations built empires, one powerful entity within the ruling establishment used its position to insinuate itself into our institutions of government, infiltrate our financial system, co-opt most of our manufacturing capability and acquire millions of acres of American farmland. They paid U.S. media outlets tens of millions of dollars each year to report fictitious news stories, invested millions in U.S. Universities and billions in support of promising local politicians which after decades matured into dozens of compromised members of Congress and eventually the White House itself.

The Chinese Communist Party is the largest multinational corporation in the world and the most powerful element of the global ruling class. They have relationships with every U.S. based multinational corporation including big tech and the defense industry. They own five of the world's six largest banks and control an extensive list of international organizations including the World Bank, World Health Organization and the Bank for International Settlements. They are natural allies in a ruling class effort to reset the global economy into a one world socialist system, a plan that depends on the dissolution of the United States as a capitalist superpower.

Trump's win in the 2016 election upset these plans. He pulled the U.S. out of the Paris Climate Accords, reversed Obama era restrictions on energy production and imposed sanctions on China. He defended U.S. citizenship at our borders and pursued trade agreements that supported American business. In response, the ruling class used the Justice Department against the President and his supporters, deployed a bio-engineered virus as an excuse to shut down the economy, and finally, conducted a thinly veiled scam election to put a China compromised dementia patient at the head of a puppet government in the United States. Someone behind the scenes has a mute button for Biden's microphone, gives him a list of reporters to call on for rehearsed questions and orders him hustled away when he goes off script. These claims sound far-fetched only if you watch the news or read social media, it's very much in character for a group of billionaires for whom the Great Depression was a business deal.

The 2020 election mirrored almost exactly what the CIA has done in a dozen countries over the last thirty years and practically the entire U.S. Congress went along with it because the Biden family's criminal dealings with China, Russia and Ukraine are not unique. The system was designed to insure that only ruling class approved candidates could become President. Trump was an outsider who wasn't supposed to be there, and he was sniffing around Joe's Ukraine deals and Hunter's laptop. His re-election would likely have resulted in investigations that would have threatened hundreds of government officials including dozens of sitting members of Congress. Most Republicans were as desperate for an "insurrection" as the Biden faction because an honest vote count was a threat to their power, if not their liberty.

In a kind of friendly rivalry among thieves, once they were sure they had gotten away with the election, the Biden camp showed a figurative middle finger to George W Bush, an amateur artist, with Hunter's half million-dollar refrigerator art. They planted the "conspiracy theory" that Hunter's art was a scheme to launder bribe money to obscure the sophisticated scheme they have used for decades to launder bribes.

Predawn raids broadcast live on sanctioned media. Political prisoners held without bail. Rigged elections, banned speech, laws ignored and police departments de-funded. It doesn't just sound like a totalitarian police state. Under Stalin's rule, police were on the lowest rung of the social ladder. They were last in line for the worst food and lived in the poorest rooms because the government claimed that equity had eliminated crime. Our leaders are using Stalin's Utopian rhetoric without even realizing it. Or are they? During the summer of 2021, Biden, while decrying some state's voting reforms, repeated Stalin's words almost verbatim. "The people who cast the votes decide nothing. The people who count the votes decide everything."

The people who elected Donald Trump are no more a threat to this country than the people who voted for Barack Obama, but they are a threat to the ruling class and that will not be tolerated. Biden's parody of a Presidency probably won't last four years and may not need to. When off the shelf Covid variants, another ten trillion in stimulus and the climate laws that were hidden in the stimulus bills take effect, the economy will collapse, the reset will commence and the fiction of our old system of government will no longer be needed.

Our "elected" representatives have been surrendering the country a few billion dollars at a time for decades. They're doing it now by the trillions because time is almost up. The United States government's own financial documents show conclusively that it is hopelessly insolvent. There is mathematically no path that avoids some form of U.S. debt default leading to a world-wide economic collapse.

We are living through the fall of the greatest nation in history and there is precious little accurate documentation of its demise. The following pages will separate the conspiracies from the theories and examine events in light of their connections and who profited from them. We will document direct connections between the conspirators from the Federal Reserve and 16th Amendment to Allen Dulles and the military industrial complex to the murder of a President, the truth behind Watergate, 9/11, Covid and the 2020 election, to the final economic collapse and dawn of a socialist world order run by a corporate hegemony dominated by Communist China.

Elected leaders and sanctioned media will keep saying everything is fine until an hour or so before store shelves are empty and gas pumps run dry. Then the ruling class will step in to save the masses. Americans living in luxury on the backs of the world's poor will be a thing of the past. There will be equity.

The Federal Reserve

The story of the fall of the United States begins with two related events in 1909. In July Congress passed the 16th Amendment to the Constitution and four months later European banking dynasties represented by the Warburgs and Rothschilds met in secret with the American dynasties of Morgan and Rockefeller at JP Morgan's Jekyll Island.

The bankers laid the framework for the establishment of a private Central Bank that they would control. In 1912 Woodrow Wilson agreed to their plan in exchange for money and support for his presidential campaign. On Christmas Eve 1913 while few were paying attention, Congress passed the Federal Reserve Act which Wilson promptly signed into law.

The Aviator, Charles Lindbergh's father was a Congressman from Minnesota at the time. Lindbergh told Congress that "*This Act establishes the most gigantic trust on Earth. When the President signs this bill, the invisible government by the Monetary Power will be legalized, the people may not know it immediately, but the day of reckoning is only a few years removed. The worst legislative crime of the ages is perpetrated by this banking bill.*" In 1917 Lindbergh brought articles of impeachment against members of the Federal Reserve Board of Governors, including Paul Warburg and William P. G. Harding, charging that they were involved "in a conspiracy to violate the Constitution and laws of the United States." Lindbergh published a book entitled Banking, Currency, and the Money Trust. In 1918 federal agents destroyed the printing plates and all copies of the book.

Three years after he signed the Federal Reserve Act, Woodrow Wilson expressed regret for his part in the scheme saying "*The growth of the nation and all our activities are in the hands of a few men. We have come to be one of the worst ruled, one of the most completely controlled and dominated governments in the civilized world. No longer a government of free opinion, no longer a government by conviction and the free vote of the majority, but a government by the opinion and duress of a small group of dominant men.*"

Article One, Section Eight of the Constitution says, *"Congress shall have the power to coin money and regulate the value thereof."* A constitutional amendment would have been required to legally give that authority to a private entity. The Federal Reserve is privately owned, and one hundred percent of its shareholders are private banks. None of its stock is owned by the government. It does not answer to voters or to any branch of government. The FED is not Federal, is not a bank, has no reserves and has no real legal authority to create money.

The Federal Reserve creates money by keying it into its balance sheet. It then loans it to the U.S. government who illegally withholds real, earned money from our wages and salaries to pay interest on a debt conjured out of thin air. Every dollar the Federal Reserve has created for over a hundred years was a direct transfer of property from the individual U.S. citizen who earned it, to the ruling elite. The Federal Reserve is a branch of a private, global corporation that has invested in both sides of every global conflict from World War II to Afghanistan. Its chairman, along with the chairs of the world's other central banks, sit on the board of the Bank for International Settlements where they key more money into that balance sheet and loan it to other banks, governments and corporations to support a growing world governing authority that by its very nature displaces the authority of U.S. citizens and supersedes our Constitution.

The Federal Reserve was created by an act of treason and Representative Lindbergh wasn't the only one who knew it.

In 1932, Representative Louis McFadden said in an address to the Congress, *"We have in this country one of the most corrupt institutions the world has ever known. When the Federal Reserve was passed, the people of the United States did not perceive that a world system was being set up here, a super-state controlled by international bankers, and international industrialists acting together to enslave the world for their own pleasure!"*

On May 23, 1933, Congressman McFadden brought impeachment charges against the members of the Federal Reserve. *"Whereas I charge them jointly and severally with having brought about a repudiation of the national currency of the United States in order that the gold value of the said currency might be given to private interests. I charge them with having arbitrarily and unlawfully taken over 80 billion dollars from the United States Government in the year 1928. I charge them with having arbitrarily and unlawfully raised and*

11

lowered the rates on money. I charge them with having brought about the decline of prices on the New York Stock Exchange, I charge them with having conspired to transfer to foreigners and international money lenders, title to and control of the financial resources of the United States. I charge them with having published false and misleading propaganda intended to deceive the American people and to cause the United States to lose its independence. I charge them with the crime of having treasonable conspired and acted against the peace and security of the United States, and with having treasonable conspired to destroy the constitutional government of the United States."

In 1937 Representative Charles Binderup called for the Government to buy all of the stock in the Federal Reserve and to create a new Board controlled by Congress. He was ousted in the next election.

In 1967, Representative Wright Patman tried to have the Federal Reserve audited. He told Congress *"In the United States we have, in effect, two governments. We have the duly constituted Government. Then we have an independent, uncontrolled and uncoordinated government in the Federal Reserve System, operating the money powers which are reserved to Congress by the Constitution."*

In 1971, Representative John Rarick introduced H.R. 351: *"To vest in the Government of the United States the full, absolute, complete, and unconditional ownership of the twelve Federal Reserve Banks."* He said: *"The Federal Reserve is not an agency of government. It is a private banking monopoly."* During the 1980s, Rep. Phil Crane of Illinois introduced House Resolution H.R. 70 that called for an annual audit of the Federal Reserve. The same year Representative Henry Gonzales introduced H.R. 1470, that called for the repeal of the Federal Reserve Act.

Ron Paul, a long-time critic of the Federal Reserve, put it best. *"To understand how unwise it is to have the Federal Reserve, one must first understand the magnitude of the privileges they have. They have been given the power to create money, by the trillions, and to give it to their friends, under any terms they wish, with little or no meaningful oversight or accountability. Thus, the loudest arguments against greater transparency are likely to come from those friends, and understandably so."*

The Federal Reserve System has never been audited, their meetings, and the minutes of those meetings, are not open or available to the public. The Federal Reserve was only half of the plan.

The 16th Amendment

Once they got a central bank with the power to coin money, the ruling class didn't need an income tax to fund government. They needed an income tax to control the people. Any time they want money, they just add it to the balance sheet of the Federal Reserve, it comes out of the economy indiscriminately. The income tax though, with its access to the country's payroll before the checks are printed, and its armed IRS enforcement agents, is much more than money, its power. For every billionaire in this country, there are one million lower, middle or upper middle-class people. The 16th Amendment was written by billionaires.

Our Constitution dictates that taxes be uniform for everyone and apportioned equally across the States specifically to prevent a state sanctioned favored class that once established, is always sustained by the inevitable serf class. The bankers who created the Federal Reserve aligned themselves with progressive politicians who had visions of a state-sponsored utopia, to give the government a prior lien on all of the labor of its subjects. The average American now works twenty years for the government simply to pay his taxes while the typical billionaire is exempted by charitable foundations, classifications like long term capital gains and income not subject to U.S. jurisdiction. The 16th Amendment is the justification for an eighty-thousand-page tax code in whose fine print can be found everything the moneyed elite ever asked for. For the rest of us, anything they do not take is a concession. The ruling class, using force and its control over the distribution of information, has convinced working Americans to accept an Internal Revenue Service with the power to confiscate their wages from their very paychecks. The amendment allegedly ratified by a majority of voters in three fourths of the States did not authorize this tax system. Voters were asked to approve a different amendment, which was then switched for the 16th Amendment that we now labor under.

As proposed in the bill Congress passed in 1909, the 16th Amendment would only apply to profit from investments, dividends, interest and capital gains. It did not, and voters were specifically told it would not apply to wages and salaries. It was sold to the American public as a way to make the rich pay their "fair share". At the time the government was funded by import taxes. These taxes gave American manufacturers a competitive edge over foreign companies which the bankers and politicians claimed allowed American companies to charge more which working people paid for. They promised the amendment would tax the profits of these rich businessmen and the interest earned by their investors. They've continued to make the same promise in every election since, and the rich pay little or no taxes to this day.

In 1913 the word income was known to mean profit from investments, dividends, interest and capital gains as opposed to wages and salaries in colloquial language and as defined in legal documents and publications of the time. Members of Congress who voted for the Amendment in 1909 and ask their constituents to ratify it stated unequivocally that it did not and would never apply to wages and salaries. Therefore, as written and as ratified, the 16th Amendment does not authorize a tax on wages and salaries. The Income Tax is illegal.

It's easy to come up with statistics that show how the top few percent of wage earners pay a large share of all federal income taxes. It's true, individuals who report very high incomes pay a lot of income taxes and the bottom 40 percent of wage earners pay little or no income taxes, but those are misleading numbers. The bottom 80 percent of wage earners work for twenty of their 45-year careers to pay taxes. The top 10 percent, and the top 1 percent that primarily comprises the ruling class, spend a lot of money that is not declared income. When they do declare income it's usually long-term capital gains, taxed at a lower rate than wages and not subject to Social Security and Medicare taxes. The only "fair" tax system is one that is simple enough to eliminate the professions of accountant and tax attorney and treats each American the same as every other, just like the Constitution prescribed.

The 16th Amendment was initially proposed in an effort to block income tax legislation, which the Supreme Court had already ruled was unconstitutional. Few believed at the time that it had any chance of being ratified and they were probably right. A former Illinois Department of Revenue investigator named Bill Benson spent two years in the 1980's, researching the ratification of the 16th Amendment. He collected thousands of certified legal documents from both state and federal archives documenting that the 16th Amendment was fraudulently declared to have been ratified by the U.S. Secretary of State, Philander Knox. Benson, and his co-researcher Red Beckman, published a book detailing each state's adoption, or rejection, of the amendment entitled, "The Law That Never Was." In 2004, the Department of Justice filed a lawsuit against Benson alleging that the book was a "fraudulent tax shelter" that violated Section 6700 of the Internal Revenue Code. Lindbergh's book was literally burned in 1918, Benson's legally burned in 2004, today they're digitally burning "misinformation" on Amazon, Facebook and Twitter.

In the years before our government became controlled by the moneyed elite, western civilization advanced at such a pace that people born in horse and buggy days lived to watch Americans walk on the Moon. That progress was driven by inventors like Tesla, the Wright brothers and Alexander Graham Bell along with massive corporations like U.S. Steel, Standard Oil and Ford Motor Company. The first multinational corporation in America was founded by a Russian immigrant who arrived penniless and became a millionaire importing bananas from South America. It wasn't until he hired the Dulles brothers, both influential U.S. government officials, to defend his company against federal intervention, that he began to overthrow South American governments.

As long as the free market was driven by freely made individual decisions, it rewarded and encouraged decent, productive behavior. Decent, productive people made the United States a country the rest of the world risked their lives to come to. When a few wealthy bankers and businessmen gained access to the use of force in the name of government, they necessarily created a serf class. Many Americans whose current and future wages were stolen, hardly noticed when a hundred years of invention, innovation and product development slowed to a trickle as an increasingly corrupt government enforced monopolies and replaced private enterprise with mandated products, an army of public employees, and assistance programs whose primary function is to expand the need for assistance programs.

Corruption is the nature of government because spending other people's money corrupts human nature. Honesty is in the nature of free enterprise because it is voluntary, to succeed you must earn the trust of your customers, suppliers and lenders. The basic genius of our system was the sanctity of private property. A political boss or bureaucrat wouldn't get away with taking what doesn't belong to him because sooner or later the people it does belong to would put a stop to it. The meritocracy of free enterprise has ended more discrimination, poverty and other societal ills like drug abuse than government programs which have failed every cause and trapped huge segments of society into violent poverty.

The income tax removed all limits on government and so had the effect of nullifying the Constitution. Its exponential growth was inevitable and unstoppable as is its demand for our ever-greater submission to the centralized will. Ford, Carnegie and Rockefeller formed corporations whose sole purpose was to exercise the power of government. The volume of money involved undermined the value of individual private property which no longer carried enough weight to influence the system. Average Americans were priced out of representative government.

By the time President Eisenhower warned that "Our toil, resources, and livelihood" as well as "the very structure of our society" were in danger from the unwarranted influence of the military-industrial complex, it was too late. Unelected bureaucrats were already receiving millions from corporations they allotted contracts to, and the families of Congressmen populated the boards of global corporations. The directors of powerful government agencies routinely traded seats with corporate executives while conglomerates secured previously unavailable oil, mineral and agricultural resources via the use of force in the name of government. CIA sponsored coups, rebellions and assassinations, often of democratically elected leaders and practically every war since WWI were part of doing business.

Allen Dulles

The official explanation of CIA malfeasance as reported by sanctioned media, is usually constrained to a ten-year period ending with the Bay of Pigs. But the events in Iran, Guatemala and Cuba were not isolated incidents, they were part of a pattern that began in 1913, continued with the creation of the CIA and continues still to this day.

In 1933, a book, purportedly written by a member of the Warburg banking dynasty, was published in Holland that detailed a series of meetings in which New York and European bankers agreed to finance the rise to power of Adolf Hitler. The author claimed that payments were made to Hitler between 1929 and 1933 totaling 32 million dollars. The Warburg family denied the claims, but their New York banking firm, Kuhn, Loeb Co. had ties to all of the alleged conspirators including Kurt von Schröder who organized the banking firms of J. Henry Schröder in London and New York, which it was learned later acted as a conduit for money funneled to Heinrich Himmler's SS organization which continued as late as 1944, while World War II was in progress and the United States was at war with Germany. Schröder also arranged the meeting at his villa between embattled German President Papen, Heinrich Himmler, Rudolf Hess and Hitler which paved the way for Hitler to be appointed Chancellor in 1933.

In 1936 Schröder and the Rockefeller's founded the Rockefeller-Schroeder bank. Allen Dulles was on the bank's board of directors for 15 years while his brother, John Foster, acted as Rockefeller's attorney. After the war, attempts to uncover the connections between New York and European bankers and the financing of Germany's military, crossed paths with Allen Dulles at every bank, oil company and government agency.

On November 9, 1942, Dulles arrived in Bern, Switzerland to head up the Office of Strategic Services operations in that country where, according to the CIA's database of declassified documents, he and former OSS agent Thomas McKittrick, president of the Bank for International Settlements and an executive with Chase Manhattan, facilitated deals between U.S. companies and NAZI Germany including aircraft engines from United Aircraft and a deal between

Prescott Bush's Union Banking Corporation and the I.G. Farben company, who produced gas for Holocaust extermination chambers. Dulles and McKittrick were also in exactly the right place to help conceal looted Nazi gold that was smuggled out of German occupied territory and hidden in numbered Swiss accounts or moved to Argentina.

After the war Dulles, as CIA director, aggressively recruited Nazi officers as secret, anti-Soviet assets, believing the Nazis' intelligence value outweighed the "moral lapses" in their service to the Third Reich. Among them were Hitler's Chief of Military Intelligence, Reinhard Gehlen, who arrived in Washington D.C. in 1945 where he met with President Truman, Dulles and General William Donovan, Director of the Office of Strategic Services. The purpose of the meeting was to plan the reorganization of the OSS into a highly efficient covert intelligence organization. By 1946 they had produced the Central Intelligence Group, renamed the Central Intelligence Agency in 1947. Dulles would resign as president of Rockefeller's Council on Foreign Relations to take his post as Director in 1952.

Gehlen also helped create the National Security Council, from which the National Security Act of 1947 was derived to protect illegal government activities, including regime change, assassination, biological weapon and mind control programs. Armed with this authority, Dulles orchestrated successful CIA led coups in Iran in 1953 and Guatemala in 1954, claiming local Communist provocateurs were threatening Western oil supplies, the Suez and Panama canals and of course, the financial interests of a host of British and American oil companies in Iran and the United Fruit Company, Sullivan & Cromwell's client in Guatemala.

President Kennedy was an outspoken advocate of African nationalism. Patrice Lumumba, an African nationalist leader in the Congo was overthrown by a CIA backed military coup and was in CIA custody when Kennedy was elected President. Dulles knew that once Kennedy was inaugurated, he would help Lumumba, so he ordered his agents to beat Lumumba to death before the inauguration. When the President learned of the murder more than a month later, witnesses said that he was visibly distraught.

Two days before his assassination President Kennedy accepted an invitation from Indonesian President Sukarno to visit that country the following spring. Kennedy may or may not have realized that his plans were threatening a long-standing covert Dulles plan to effect regime change in Indonesia and gain unimpeded access to vast natural resources that Dulles had kept secret from Kennedy, who thought Indonesia was lacking in natural resources.

Dulles knew that if Kennedy, who was extremely popular in Indonesia, visited Sukarno, it would deal a death blow to his plan to oust the Indonesian President, install a CIA replacement (Suharto), exterminate alleged communists, and secure the archipelago for Rockefeller controlled oil and mining interests for whom he had fronted since the 1920s.

Of course, JFK never went to Indonesia in 1964, and his strategy to bring Indonesia to America's side and to ease tensions in the Cold War died with the President. Kennedy's proposed withdrawal from Vietnam, which depended on his success in Indonesia, was quickly reversed by Lyndon Johnson after JFK's execution.

Dulles ordered assassinations of undesirables abroad, destabilized foreign governments and integrated high-level Nazi intelligence agents into the CIA. His MKUltra mind control program, a continuation of experiments begun in German concentration camps, started in 1953 and went off the CIA's books in 1973 after then director Richard Helms ordered all the records destroyed. It continued disguised as academic research funded through grants from CIA front organizations which, over the next fifty years extended tentacles into everything from university and government Bio-labs to technology start-ups and pharmaceutical companies. It financed work on mind control, virus manipulation and even media-generated cognitive maps for manipulating how populations interpret events.

Little was learned of the program's successes owing to the destruction of records, but a Congressional inquiry in the 1970's heard testimony that one of MKUltra's original goals was to create a "Manchurian Candidate" style subject, although in a real world setting you would probably need to rig an election to actually get such a person into the White House.

When Kennedy fired him after the Bay of Pigs invasion, Dulles moved his operation to a remote CIA facility called "The Farm" in northern Virginia. That's where he was when Kennedy was executed, and when Jack Ruby killed Lee Harvey Oswald. In the weeks leading up to the assassination, Dulles received several visitors at his Virginia command center including William Harvey, the head of the CIA's assassination unit and Howard Hunt who later came under suspicion during the House Select Committee on Assassination hearings. Witnesses placed William Harvey in Dallas in November of 1963. Under the JFK Records Act, the CIA was compelled by federal law to release all documents related to the Kennedy assassination. Among other items missing from the released material were travel vouchers and motel receipts that could have placed William Harvey in Dallas at the time of the assassination.

It should have been obvious that an agency designed to operate outside the law, which could assassinate elected leaders and overturn democratic elections, would not restrict itself to foreign activities. Especially when viewed in light of the pattern of events which have guided the United States since 1913.

Allen Dulles was a Founding member of the Rockefeller Council on Foreign Relations, Chairman of the Board of the Rockefeller Foundation, Board Chairman of the Carnegie Endowment for International Peace, Director of the J. Henry Schroeder bank in London, Director of (Rothschild-affiliated) Kuhn, Loeb & Company, and Director of Sullivan & Cromwell who had brokered deals for J.P. Morgan, Andrew Carnegie and J.D. Rockefeller since the 1880's. He wielded immense power and his affiliation with every successor to the 1913 banking cabal make it clear on whose behalf he wielded it. They stopped letting minor interferences like elections and the Constitution get in their way a long time ago

Kennedy Assassination

After sixty years of speculation including hundreds of books on the subject, we may never know the whole truth about JFK's murder, but there are five facts that are beyond doubt.

The two men who had the greatest reason to hate Kennedy, and had the most to gain from his death, also ran the investigation into his murder.

Six decades later, intelligence agencies are still concealing documents about the assassination.

Frames 312, 313 and 314 of the Zapruder film show conclusively that the fatal headshot did not come from the sixth floor of the Texas School Book Depository.

The Warren Commission report was a blatant effort to mislead the American public, and the media covered for them.

They are still lying to us. And that's why this is still important.

These facts along with information that has been released or uncovered in the years since, together with biographies of American businessmen, government officials and politicians from the time, bring certain connections into focus.

In the 1950's and 60's, using the threat of communism to justify illegal actions, the intelligence arm of the military industrial complex was involved in deposing elected governments all over the world so that several large corporations could gain access to forced labor, energy and mineral reserves worth billions of dollars.

Today they are using the threat of terrorism, even turning it against so called domestic terrorists, to justify illegal activities worth trillions to corporations whose global interests are opposed to those of the citizens of the United States. The media is still covering for them.

The two men with motive and opportunity for Kennedy's murder, and who took an active role in its cover-up, were Lyndon Johnson and

Allen Dulles. They were from opposite political parties, but answered to the same corporate, political and banking interests.

Lyndon Johnson had a history of illegal activity and questionable associations before Deep State operatives rigged the 1948 Democratic nomination to the Senate on his behalf. He was certified the winner by 87 votes out of 988,295 cast, tens of thousands of which were later determined to be fraudulent.

His first election to Congress was financed in part by a Texas road and dam building firm called Brown & Root. By 1940 Brown & Root had already begun receiving federal contracts and at the age of 32, after having served in the House for only three years Johnson was the largest fundraiser in Congress, funneling money through the Democratic Congressional Campaign Committee to Democrat congressional races all over the country.

Some Democratic candidates received more money than had ever been spent on a congressional campaign before while other, sitting Democrat congressmen were blacklisted. Johnson was put in office as part of a wider scheme to gain influence in Congress for the same powerful moneyed interests that funded Allen Dulles' off the books assassinations and mind control experiments.

Johnson was extremely proud to the point of arrogance. No one could understand why he gave up his powerful position as leader of the Senate to accept the vice-presidential slot on Kennedy's ticket. It was assumed that Kennedy needed Johnson to carry Texas, which he would need to beat Nixon, but that doesn't explain why Johnson would accept the demotion, besides the two men despised each other. Johnson was put on the ticket by the same people who helped Kennedy win the election. It was a common ruling class tactic both as insurance, and for getting someone into the Presidency who was too crooked, inept or both, to be a viable candidate for the office.

One of Johnson's first acts when he came into the office of Vice President was to draft an executive order that by all indications, he expected Kennedy to sign. Among other powers it granted him "general supervision" over all national security matters. There is also written and audio evidence that he believed he would be given an office adjacent to the Oval Office with a White House staff of his own.

Instead, after taking office the Kennedy's and their staff blatantly snubbed Johnson at every turn. Why did Johnson assume he would be granted these powers? He wouldn't have, and he wouldn't have accepted the position if he didn't have good reason to believe that he would wield more power than a typical Vice President.

Johnson had taken office expecting a place on Air Force One with the President. Not only was he relegated to Air Force Two, but Kennedy also grounded the Boeing 707 that was supposed to serve this purpose and forced the Vice President to use an older prop plane. Johnson seemed to accept the snubs with uncharacteristic humility, but behind the scenes, Joesph Kennedy was fielding calls from irate mobsters, bankers and business leaders demanding to know what his kid thought he was doing.

Kennedy resisted the pressure and continued to disrupt the plans of some powerful people. Attorney General Robert Kennedy went after organized crime figures who had worked with the CIA in their attempt to kill Castro. The President began pulling troops out of Vietnam, started talks with the President of Indonesia, snubbed Vice President Johnson, authorized the Treasury Department to issue silver certificates and fired Allen Dulles as CIA Director. When Dulles left the Directors office, he set up shop in a CIA covert operations center in Virginia which is where he was on November 22, 1963.

The case for Oswald being the lone gunman, with its uncanny marksmanship, magic bullets and discounted witnesses was unlikely enough before Johnson's Secret Service destroyed evidence in the car and snatched the body from legal authorities before an autopsy could be performed. (Under U.S. law, the Dallas police had jurisdiction.) Then Oswald who had worked for the CIA, is killed by Jack Ruby who also worked for the CIA who then dies a short time later of cancer, leaving his family a small fortune that didn't seem to have any source.

Then came the Warren Commission. Johnson installed Allen Dulles as chief investigator and then picked Chief Justice Warren to give it an appearance of respectability. The President of the World Bank was even on the Commission. Which begs the question, why would people with as much public trust as Warren, McCloy and Gerald Ford go along with such an absurd story and obvious cover-up?

In a taped telephone conversation Johnson told Senator Richard Russell "Warren told me he wouldn't do it under any circumstances. He came down here and told me no, twice. And I just pulled out what Hoover told me about a little incident in Mexico City. And he started crying and he said, I'll just do whatever you say."

Warren was compromised and Dulles, an expert in assassinations, would have been considered a prime suspect by any standard police methodology. FBI Director Hoover's proclivity for blackmail is well documented and Ford's later role in Watergate, "We gave Nixon no choice but Ford" connects him with the conspirators. Others on the commission could have been coerced or blackmailed, but the fix was already in. They might have just been convinced that the truth was more dangerous.

While Johnson and Dulles had motive to kill Kennedy, so did their ruling class associates, which explains why the World Bank was involved. Once in office, Johnson worked assiduously to undo the damage Kennedy had done to their globalist's plans beginning with committing U.S. troops to defend the Republic of South Vietnam, an almost single-handed creation of the C.I.A.

Five months before his death, President Kennedy signed Executive Order 11110 with the intention of stripping the Federal Reserve Bank of its power to loan money to the United States Federal Government at interest. This order gave the Treasury Department the explicit authority "to issue silver certificates against any silver bullion, silver, or standard silver dollars in the Treasury" without going through the privately owned Federal Reserve Bank.

As a result, more than $4 billion in United States Notes were brought into circulation in $2 and $5 denominations. Although $10 and $20 United States Notes were never circulated, they were being printed by the Treasury Department when Kennedy was assassinated. Johnson had them destroyed and killed the program.

Joseph

Joseph Kennedy owned a warehouse building in Chicago that was so big that until 1988 it had its own zip code. The massive amount of goods that moved through the building gave Kennedy connections with unions and through them organized crime figures which controlled union membership and their massive pension funds. He became one of America's most powerful men by cornering the rum market and producing Hollywood movies in the 1930's. He used connections in the worlds of finance, politics, unions, entertainment, and organized crime to get his son elected president in 1960.

During the campaign, Kennedy used his friendship with Frank Sinatra to set up a meeting with Sam Giancana, one of America's most powerful organized crime figures, to bring mob and union money into the campaign. In exchange Kennedy agreed that his son would stop harassing organized crime syndicates, get rid of Fidel Castro and return the nationalized Cuban casinos to their previous owners, one of which was Giancana.

Washington Post editor Ben Bradlee later revealed that on election night, Chicago Mayor, Richard Daly, telephoned Kennedy and said, "Mr. President, with a little bit of luck and the help of a few close friends, you're going to win Illinois." Kennedy won Illinois and its 27 Electoral College votes by fewer than 9,400 votes. An unbelievable 89 percent of Illinois voters had cast ballots. Nixon won most of the rural counties, but Kennedy won four times his predicted lead in Chicago. Kennedy won other strong union cities in Nevada, South Carolina, and Pennsylvania which all had unbelievably high turnouts in metropolitan areas.

Out of 63 million votes cast, Kennedy won by fewer than 119,000 votes. Nixon, Kennedy and just about everyone else involved in politics or the media knew what had gone down. In some Illinois precincts more people voted for Kennedy than there were people. Nixon later wrote in his memoirs that if he had challenged the results, he would be branded a sore loser and his political career would have been over.

CIA documents released in 2007 confirmed that Giancana and Santo Trafficante Jr., the Tampa syndicate boss and one of the most powerful mobsters in pre-revolution Cuba, were paid by Allen Dulles to assassinate Fidel Castro. The night before Giancana was supposed to testify at the Select Committee on Assassinations of the US Congress, he was shot in the back of the head while cooking peppers in his home.

Robert

If Bobby Kennedy were alive today, he would have probably been a Republican. He believed the federal government had been infiltrated by socialists and communists. He worked with Senator Joe McCarthy who he saw as a brave and principled patriot whose cause was morally just, and who was vilified for seeking to do the right thing. He was a conservative who had eleven children and was opposed to militant feminism and gay liberation. In speeches and articles, he attacked the New Deal, the welfare state, counter-productive federal anti-poverty programs, and big government. By 1968, Kennedy was under attack by people who would later be seen as the fathers of the modern Democrat party, Mark Rudd, Tom Hayden, Jane Fonda, Bill Ayers and Bernardine Dohrn among others.

Allen Dulles and Prescott Bush were good friends. The elder Bush, in a letter to Dulles dated just months after Robert Kennedy's assassination expressed his hatred for the Kennedy brothers. Senator Kennedy was murdered a few hours after he was declared the winner in the South Dakota and California Democrat primaries in the 1968 presidential election. Robert Kennedy had made no bones about the fact that he intended to get to the bottom of his brother's murder after he got elected. He had also told supporters that if elected, he intended to end the Vietnam war and abolish the CIA.

Sirhan Sirhan was a nut who was not happy with Kennedy over his support for Israel. According to dozens of witnesses, on the night Kennedy was murdered, Sirhan was positioned several feet in front of Senator Kennedy, who was moving toward him. As Kennedy stopped to shake hands with hotel employees, Sirhan walked toward him extending his arm and began firing wildly, hitting five bystanders and putting two bullets in the ceiling. Forensic evidence, undisputed but not used as evidence in the trial, indicated that Senator Kennedy was hit by three bullets, fired in an upward angle from behind, by a weapon pressed up against his back with the fatal shot fired about an inch behind his right ear. The shots left powder burns on the back of his jacket and on his skin behind his right ear.

Sirhan's lawyer, who did not use the forensic evidence in defense of his client, gave the following closing argument at Sirhan's trial. "Now, let me state at the outset that I want this to sink in if anything sinks in, we are not here to free a guilty man. We tell you as we always have, that he is guilty of having killed Senator Kennedy. we expect that under the evidence in this case, whether Mr. Sirhan likes it or not, under the facts of this case, he deserves to spend the rest of his life in the penitentiary. Don't we know from dozens and dozens of witnesses that this defendant pulled the trigger that killed Senator Kennedy? There is no question about that. I wouldn't want Sirhan Sirhan to be turned loose as he is dangerous, especially when the psychiatrists tell us that he is going to get worse, and he is getting worse. There is a good Sirhan and a bad Sirhan and the bad Sirhan is nasty. We as lawyers owe the obligation to do what we think is right to the fullest extent of our ability, but we also owe an obligation to society. And I, for one, am not going to ask you to do otherwise than to bring in a verdict of guilty in the second degree."

Sirhan's revolver held a maximum of eight bullets. Kennedy was shot four times. One behind the right ear, a second near the right armpit, a third just below the right armpit and a fourth that went through Kennedy's jacket but did not hit his body. Five other people were shot in addition to Kennedy, one of whom was shot twice. That is a total of ten bullets. Additionally, witnesses and photographs reveal that several ceiling tiles were pierced by bullets, making it impossible that Sirhan was the only gunman.

Kennedy was surrounded by supporters and reporters. There were flashbulbs going off all around him, but no pictures have ever been found showing who was behind Kennedy when he was killed. Even under hypnosis, Sirhan has never been able to remember the shooting. Dr Herbert Spiegel, a world authority on hypnosis at Columbia University, said he believed Sirhan may have been hypnotized at the time of the shooting.

After all the unanswered questions surrounding John Kennedy's murder, Bobby's murder should have received scrutiny. A majority of Americans were suspicious of the official story, but the authorities and most of the media dutifully asserted that another disturbed lone gunman was responsible. The same CIA backed magazines that had spread some of the more outlandish conspiracies five years earlier, covered for sanctioned media and discouraged questions.

John Kennedy, who had more mistresses than Bill Clinton, from Marilyn Monroe to Mafia molls to White House interns from a private college prep school for girls down the road in Connecticut, was remembered by history as one of America's greatest Presidents. He might have been if his peace initiatives and fight against the Federal Reserve had come to fruition. As it was, his most notable accomplishment was forcing the withdrawal of Soviet missiles from Cuba which it turns out, was done in exchange for the withdrawal of U.S. missiles from Turkey and a secret pledge to let Castro and the communists keep Cuba. He then allowed the military establishment to convinced him to deploy sixteen thousand troops to Vietnam where Eisenhower had resisted pressure from the Joint Chiefs and only sent six hundred advisers. As soon as our troops arrived, covert C.I.A. operatives, in a move designed to trap Kennedy into the war, orchestrated a coup in which our ally, President Ngo Dinh Diem, was assassinated. When Kennedy responded by working on a regional peace deal to end the war, he was assassinated, which allowed Lyndon Johnson to send what would end up being almost a million U.S. troops into Vietnam where over 55,000 were killed in exchange for absolutely nothing of value to the United States.

Watergate

Eisenhower's warning about the military industrial complex is a clue that his administration was not comfortable with the powerful forces that had taken hold within his government. By the time his Vice President took office a decade later, there were 535,000 U.S. troops in Vietnam and the military hierarchy wanted more.

Four years later, Richard Nixon, who history has recorded among our country's worst Presidents, had withdrawn all U.S. troops and brought home the POWs. He also ended the draft, gave 18-year-olds the right to vote, created the Environmental Protection Agency, the Cancer Institute, the Occupational Health and Safety Administration and desegregated 70 percent of all Southern public schools. He negotiated SALT I and the ABM treaty with Russia limiting intercontinental ballistic missiles armed with nuclear weapons, ended decades of hostility between the U.S. and China, rescued Israel in the Yom Kippur War, and recruited Egypt out of the Soviet bloc into being a U.S. ally.

By 1972, his successes won him a 49-state landslide, but they threatened the ruling class establishment who still controlled the culture, media, bureaucracy and Congress. When he became President, Nixon and Henry Kissinger bypassed the State Department cutting the military industrial complex/ruling class out of the decision-making process. His "New Federalism" philosophy of devolving power to state and local governments ran counter to the centralized power needs of the ruling class. Nixon was far too popular for his re-election to be prevented in 1972, so they needed another method of removing him from office. Their third world assassination techniques had aroused too much suspicion after two high-profile killings in five years, so they devised something only slightly more nuanced for Nixon.

Nixon's Vice President, Spiro Agnew, was easy to get rid of since he had taken kickbacks from contractors during his time as Baltimore County Executive and Governor of Maryland. Agnew's replacement was hand-picked by the ruling class. According to The New York Times, when Nixon needed to replace Agnew, he "sought advice from senior Congressional leaders." The advice was unanimous. "We gave Nixon no choice but Ford," House Speaker Carl Albert said later.

Ford's involvement in the Kennedy assassination cover-up should have made Nixon wary, but less than a year after winning a 49-state landslide, he had illusions of invincibility.

Five burglars were arrested at the Watergate offices of the Democratic National Committee on June 17, 1972. James W. McCord was a former FBI and CIA agent. Virgilio R. Gonzales was a Cuban refugee. Frank A. Sturgis had CIA connections and involvement in anti-Castro activities. Bernard L. Barker was a former CIA operative. Eugenio R. Martinez was an active, on the payroll CIA agent. E. Howard Hunt, later arrested for planning the Watergate burglary, was Executive Assistant to Allen Dulles and had also supervised the five burglars during the Bay of Pigs invasion.

They all worked for the CIA during the Bay of Pigs. The same five people who worked for Allen Dulles at the time Lee Harvey Oswald and Jack Ruby worked for Dulles. The Same Allen Dulles who President Kennedy fired as CIA Director. The same Allen Dulles who President Johnson later named head investigator for the Warren Commission to find the "truth" about Kennedy's assassination.

The fact that Martinez was actively being paid by the CIA at the time of the arrests wasn't confirmed until 2017 when the CIA finally complied with a 1995 FOIA request by dumping 12 million pages onto the CIA's Freedom of Information Act Electronic Reading Room website. The pages also contained official memoranda of record and telephone call transcripts by key government officials describing the interaction of senior CIA officials with the Department of Justice, the FBI and White House staff including that Lieutenant General Vernon Walters, the Deputy Director of the CIA, met with Acting Director Patrick Gray of the FBI on July 12, 1972, to discuss assistance the CIA had provided to retired CIA officer E. Howard Hunt, of the White House Special Investigations Unit ("The Plumbers").

In all the coverage of two of the biggest political stories in U.S. history, the sanctioned media helped to cover up direct CIA involvement in Watergate and the connections between Kennedy's assassination and Watergate. Then Nixon's hand-picked ruling class successor and Warren Commission co-conspirator, fired Nixon's CIA Director William Colby, who had been cooperating with congressional investigations into coups, attempted coups, and murder plots in Iran, Cuba and Chile among other places.

Ford named George H. W. Bush as Colby's replacement at the CIA. Bush didn't have any evident qualifications for the job, especially at a time when the agency was under such intense scrutiny. Bush's resume consisted of being U.N. ambassador, Republican National Committee chairman, and the U.S. envoy to Beijing, where both Nixon and Kissinger ignored him.

September 11, 2001

We were attacked by Al-Qaeda terrorists from Saudi Arabia. We watched as they flew planes full of people into those buildings. We were never told that the hijackers were financed and assisted by agents of the Saudi Royal Family who arranged and paid for their boarding in the United States, English lessons and flying lessons. The Saudi terrorists killed Americans and knocked down buildings, but that was not the object of their attacks. They were after something less tangible and much more valuable. The source of America's greatness is the liberty of its people. The Constitution codified and protected a space for liberty to grow. Al-Qaeda attacked that space. The resilience of our system depended on how our government responded to the attacks, but our government was controlled by people who wanted that space for themselves, so 9/11 was used to make another massive shift towards authoritarianism.

Conspiracy theorists were used again to discourage questions and protect the official explanation. The ruling establishment spread the story that Larry Silverstein bought terrorism insurance two months before the attacks, when it was debunked by sanctioned media, all challenges to the official explanation were said to be settled. You can't lease a 4.5 billion dollar building without buying insurance and the industry didn't start excluding terrorism until after 9/11. Since that theory was debunked, the official explanation, conveniently wrapped in our flag, cannot be questioned. As with the Kennedy executions, the cover-up is incidental to the real goal, the people must accept without complaint the explanation of our rulers.

The thread that stretches from 1913 to the coming economic collapse and its consequences, run through 9/11 and its aftermath. George W Bush acted as the direct decedent and benefactor of his great grandfather Samuel's connections to the Warburgs, Rothschilds, Morgans and Rockefellers. Samuel Bush ran John Rockefeller's Buckeye Steel Corporation before gaining a position on the War Industries Board where he awarded Rockefeller's Remington Arms Company 69 percent of government small arms contracts during WWI. George W's grandfather Prescott and his father-in-law George Herbert Walker, through connections with the Warburgs became managing directors of Brown Brothers Harrington and Union Banking Corporation which financed Adolf Hitler before and during World War II. Profits from Prescott's Nazi investments directly benefited George W, who by September 2001 had deep ties through his father to the CIA, the Saudi Royal family and to a consortium of oil companies that had lobbied the U.S. government for an invasion of Iraq and Afghanistan since at least 1997.

In the days following 9/11, the Bush administration helped the bin Laden family escape without answering questions. Less than two months later, Bush signed the Patriot Act, the first of many laws that allow our government to spy on American citizens, monitor phone and email communications, collect bank and credit reporting records, track Internet activity, search private property without a warrant and eventually hold political prisoners in solitary confinement for months on end for supporting the wrong candidate. Less than a year later he created a new Domestic Security/Secret Police force misleadingly called the Department of Homeland Security.

Years later, our government in the person of James Clapper, Director of National Intelligence, testified under oath before Congress that his agency was not spying on "millions or hundreds of millions of Americans". Three months after that, when Edward Snowden leaked classified documents that proved Clapper lied, a warrant was issued for Snowden's arrest. Clapper got a job with CNN. In less than a decade, the Al-Qaeda terrorists who helped plan the 9/11 attacks, were running Afghanistan and the U.S. Secret Police were forcing injections and face coverings on American citizens.

United Press International, September 2, 2003. "The bin Laden family were granted extraordinary White House privileges to fly out of U.S. airspace following the attacks. At least four flights with about 160 Saudi Nationals, including two-dozen members of the bin Laden family, flew to Saudi Arabia that week without even being interviewed by the FBI."

Two days after 9/11, Saudi Arabia's ambassador to the U.S., Prince Bandar, met with President Bush at the White House. Over the next few days, the Saudis were allowed to collect more than 160 Saudi officials, including relatives of Osama bin Laden, from around the U.S. and fly them on chartered jets to Saudi Arabia. The FBI escorted some of them to the airport. Could it have anything to do with the fact that decades earlier, the Saudi Royal Family had invested money in George H W's CIA/oil business? We can't ask. Prince Bandar went on to run his country's intelligence agency.

Thousands of documents concerning the attacks are still classified over twenty years later. It has leaked that some of them show that Saudi Arabia financed the attacks. Documents released by the FBI reveal that Saudi government officials prepared for the hijackers' arrival, gave them money, places to live and arranged for English and flying lessons. It makes you wonder what else the classified documents are hiding and why the official story would be endangered by their release.

It is unpatriotic to question the official explanation that a handful of young Saudi Arabians who came neither from Iraq nor from Afghanistan, outwitted the CIA, the FBI, all sixteen US intelligence agencies and all of our ally's intelligence agencies including Israel's Mossad, which is believed to have penetrated every terrorist organization on the planet. This handful of non-English speaking Arabs who arrived in the U.S. never having seen the cockpit of an airplane, are supposed to have outwitted the National Security Council, the State Department, NORAD and got past airport security four times within an hour on the same morning, then prevented the US Air Force from launching interceptor aircraft, and caused three modern steel and concrete buildings, including one not hit by an airplane, to collapse into their own footprints.

By 11:00 AM the same day, the Bush Administration announced that Osama bin Laden was responsible and by 11:00 PM declared Afghanistan a state sponsor of terror. Four weeks later the U.S. commenced a full-scale invasion of Afghanistan which would have required four months to prepare.

Robert Mueller was a loyal ruling class soldier long before the Russia Hoax. As Bush's FBI Director he began work immediately after 9/11 to cover up Saudi Arabia's role. Former Sen. Bob Graham of Florida said that Mueller personally intervened to cut off inquiry regarding Saudi assistance to the hijackers. A former FBI agent, Stephen K. Moore, also confirmed Saudi complicity. If Bush wasn't in on the planning, he was certainly part of the cover-up. Considering that our government is holding six hundred or so citizens in prison for trespassing on January 6th, giving Bush the benefit of the doubt should be considered an unequal application of the law.

A lot has been made about the way the buildings collapsed, as if demolition engineers had brought them straight down. The official story is that heat from the fires weakened the damaged steel structure until the weight of the floors above came down, crushing subsequent floors like domino's falling. If that's what happened, it shouldn't have.

The Empire State building was constructed in thirteen and a half months beginning on March 17, 1930. As the steel structure was constructed, hundreds of bricklayers covered the framework in fireproof bricks so that in case of fire, it wouldn't weaken and threaten the integrity of the building. In 1945, a B-25 bomber on its way to Newark Airport in New Jersey crashed into the 79th floor. The Empire State Building suffered minor damage.

It would be easier to accept that fire caused the towers to collapse if it wasn't for World Trade Center Building Seven. It was not struck by an airplane, yet it inexplicably collapsed into its own footprint hours after the attack. The National Institute of Standards and Technology, NIST claimed that embers from the burning Twin Towers ignited a fire which then caused the 47-story building to collapse on itself. No steel framed building before or since has collapsed because of fire.

Nineteen years after 9/11, a group of 3,000 engineers, scientists and architects demanded that the NIST retract and correct its 2008 report that concluded building seven collapsed because fire weakened the steel supporting it. The group makes no assertion as to why it may have been a "controlled demolition" and says its only interest is in ensuring that there's no need to rethink the structural steel design of high-rise buildings because the design was not at fault.

University of Alaska Fairbanks civil engineering professor Leroy Hulsey, principal investigator, his research assistants, Feng Xiao, an associate professor at Nanjing University of Science and Technology and Zhili Quan, a bridge engineer for the South Carolina Department of Transportation, found that the design standard of the building was not exceeded by the fire and that simultaneous and controlled demolition caused the structural steel to fail. "The bottom line is that the NIST report is flawed and of no value to future engineering or architectural learning."

A detailed four-year analysis by the team at UAF said that the building seven collapse was a "near-simultaneous failure of every column in the building" and dismissed the NIST finding that heat from the fire caused beams to "walk off" their moorings. The report stated "Fires could not have caused weakening or displacement of structural members capable of initiating any of the hypothetical local failures alleged to have triggered the total collapse of the building. "Nor could any local failures, even if they had occurred, have triggered a sequence of failures that would have resulted in the observed total collapse."

The NIST is lying, Saudi Arabia's role in the attacks was covered up and the United States invaded Iraq and Afghanistan under false pretenses. If we accept the official story without question, it is because it's no longer our place to question our leaders.

Iraq and Afghanistan

On January 28, 1998, the Project For A New American Century wrote a letter to President Clinton proposing a preemptive invasion of Iraq and overthrow of Saddam Hussein to protect a "significant portion of the world's supply of oil."

The signatures on that letter included those of Dick Cheney, Donald Rumsfeld, John Bolton, Paul Wolfowitz, Elliott Abrams, Richard L. Armitage, Richard Perle, William J. Bennett, Robert Kagan, Zalmay Khalilzad, William Kristol, and Robert B. Zoellick. All of whom joined the George W. Bush administration and used 9/11 as an excuse for the invasion they had planned years earlier.

Iraq had been a counter to Iran ever since the U.S. government helped Saddam into power. It was one of the most secular countries in the Middle East, had women in high office, and did not sympathize with Al-Qaeda or Bin-laden. The Bush administration knew that Iraq had no weapons of mass destruction, UN inspectors had been searching for WMD in Iraq for weeks. After over 400 unhindered inspections of government facilities, Saddam's palaces even caves, they found nothing.

The bi-partisan war (Hillary and Obama voted for it in the Senate) was orchestrated by Former Secretary of State, James Baker who was counsel to the Bush family, ExxonMobil and the House of Saud, who were part of a corporate-military-industrial conglomerate working to keep world oil production levels steady, prices up and oil traded in dollars. Saddam was a threat because he was selling Iraq's oil outside of the consortium's Saudi/OPEC restrictions and he was selling it for Euros, not dollars.

Baker and Vice President Cheney drafted a 323-page plan for the State Department that included sending ex-Shell Oil CEO Phil Carroll to Baghdad to take charge of Iraq's oil. Carroll then passed off control of Iraq's oil to Bob McKee of Halliburton, who immediately stopped trading oil in Euros and cut Iraq oil production to under OPEC(Saudi) limits.

4,497 Americans died to accomplish this.

In 1997 a group of oil companies, including Unocal, Amoco, Exxon and Pennzoil were trying to figure out how to get 200 billion barrels of oil and more than 236 trillion cubic feet of natural gas reserves from Turkmenistan, Uzbekistan, and Kazakhstan to world markets.

There were three possible routes. Across China, which would require a 5,000 mile plus pipeline through territory controlled by the Chinese Communist Party, through Iran, where U.S. companies were prohibited by U.S. Sanctions, or through Afghanistan and Pakistan to the port at Karachi.

On February 12, 1998, a representative from the group, John Maresca, vice president for international relations of the Unocal Corporation, speaking to the House Subcommittee on Asia and the Pacific of the Committee on International Relations, mentioned repeatedly that the group "could not begin construction of a pipeline "until an internationally recognized Afghanistan Government is in place."

In the months that followed, several Committee members received rather large campaign contributions and several positions that had opened up on the boards of Unocal, Amoco, Exxon and Pennzoil were filled with the advice of the same members of Congress.

On October 15, 1999, the UN Security Council adopted Resolution 1267, creating the al-Qaeda and Taliban Sanctions Committee, and covert U.S. military activities in Afghanistan began. May 15, 2001, Vice President Cheney's Energy Task Force submitted a report naming the Caspian regions oil and gas reserves as "of strategic national security importance." To the United States.

September 9, 2001, the Bush Administration finalized the Afghanistan invasion plan. October 7, 2001, George W. Bush announced the beginning of Afghanistan invasion. June 13, 2002, former Unocal consultant Hamid Karzai is elected President of Afghanistan. December 27, 2002, the Afghanistan pipeline deal is signed.

2,216 Americans died for that pipeline.

Over the ensuing years we learned that the Enron study that estimated the Turkmenistan, Uzbekistan, and Kazakhstan oil reserves at 200 billion barrels was greatly exaggerated and that the oil in question was of very low quality. Dick Cheney's prediction that the

United States would be importing 80 percent of its energy by 2020 was off by... 80 percent. The resulting decrease in energy profits reduced oil industry lobbying budgets. Having grown fat on oil money, members of Congress and other decision makers in Washington couldn't curb their appetites to save their country, so the Chinese Communist Party made up the shortfall.

In August of 2021 the Department of Homeland Security issued a bulletin naming the two greatest terrorist threats facing our nation. "Opposition to Covid measures" and "Claims of election fraud". While D.H.S. was chasing down mask-less Trump voters, the Afghan army we had spent twenty years training and equipping, were taking off their uniforms and reporting to their Taliban leaders. When we invaded Afghanistan in 2001, the Taliban were armed with small arms fired primarily from horseback. When our troops pulled out twenty years later, the Taliban had a modern military including an air force with U.S. trained pilots. The generals and the State Department told us that the Afghan army we had trained and armed could handle the Taliban. As U.S. troops followed orders to retreat, we learned that the army we had trained *were* the Taliban, and now they have the third most well-equipped military on the planet behind only the United States and China.

The U.S. Navy's most advanced Gerald R. Ford class, nuclear powered aircraft carriers, still under construction in 2021, cost 12 billion dollars each. We left enough armaments behind in Afghanistan to pay for seven of them.

One of the first things Trump did after he was elected was meet with the Generals who run our military. After meeting with the Joint Chiefs for over an hour he told them that if he had just bought a company and found that it was being run by as incompetent a group of losers as were running the U.S. military, he would fire them all and start over. What Trump didn't yet realize, was that they weren't just incompetent, they were traitors. They didn't answer to the President of the United States, they worked for the ruling class. They took orders from Morgan Stanley and Boeing Aerospace. They worked to damage Trump's Presidency and undermined his authority for four years.

Arming the Taliban was no more an accident than when the C.I.A. armed rebels in Nicaragua during the 1980's. It was another part of the pattern that began in 1913 of deliberately undermining representative government both in the United States and elsewhere. It was giving aid to the enemy of the United States while at the same time declaring U.S. citizens to be a threat to national security. After the 2020 election, military leaders met with Biden officials to discuss the possible military takeover of government if Trump challenged the election results. Because of concerns raised at that meeting, the U.S. military began a purge of possible Trump supporters immediately after Biden's inauguration.

Climate Change

"The entire North polarized cap will disappear in five years" Al Gore, 2008

The science of global climate has been extensively studied for over 150 years and is well understood. If there is a mystery, it is that the extraordinarily complicated balance between millions of variables ranging from the speed of the Earths spin to the nature of atoms and the chemical bonds that hold a molecule together, are so precisely arranged so as to maintain a relatively steady global temperature in the range of liquid water.

The science of climate change as it relates to human activity has also been extensively studied, is well understood and bears no resemblance to the information being disseminated in our schools, sanctioned media, by elected officials and scientists from other disciplines who should know better than to lend their credentials to theories they have not studied.

The Climate Change political movement has predicted that the Polar caps would be gone by 2013, Miami would be under water by 2015 and entire nations would be wiped off the Earth by 2020. None of it happened and yet in 2021, our government took billions from working Americans and gave it to six or seven multinational corporations to build electric cars while enforcing regulations that make it impossible for non-subsidized businesses to build cars that could actually replace the combustion engine.

All of the evidence for impending disaster or an "existential threat" consists of models of the extraordinarily complicated balance mentioned above in which minute adjustments to assumptions cause a wide range of outcomes of which the likelihood of future funding seems to be the deciding factor. All of the actual measurements of global temperatures, sea levels, ice packs and ocean temperatures have invalidated the "existential threat" claims.

A good scientific theory should accurately describe observations and make definite predictions about the results of future observations. Scientists have successfully satisfied neither of these requirements in regard to Climate Change, and on those grounds the political movement wants us to sacrifice U.S. energy independence and world economic superiority based on the vague assumption that the predictions will surely come true sooner or later. Meanwhile, the movement's most ardent supporters travel the planet in private jets and build multi-million-dollar homes on the shores of the Atlantic and Pacific oceans.

The income tax and Federal Reserve were designed to establish a favored class, supported by a serf class. The Climate Change movement was designed to force a more basic form of submission by the serf class, the elimination of individual transportation.

Almost without exception the nations of Earth pollute at a rate inverse to the success of their economies. The wealthier the nation, the less it pollutes. Free enterprise is the most successful economic system man has ever produced and is the best hope for the planet's future. The Climate Change political movement is part of a plan, together with a world banking system and world health organization, to establish a socialist world government. To the extent that they succeed, the planet will suffer.

The U.S. has cut carbon emissions by twenty percent in fifteen years primarily because of private sector innovation in the natural gas industry. The Climate Change movement has no intention of replacing every fossil fueled vehicle with electric. They'll ban the combustion engine, but there's no plan to replace it. They are intentionally stifling all of the other alternatives to gas and diesel by mandating electric while shutting down fossil fuel production so they can control the population's ability to move around without permission.

Electric cars use the same amount of energy to move a given weight as a gas-powered car. The only difference is the method by which the energy is delivered to the drive wheels. A Tesla Model 3 has 900 pounds of oil and gas in its materials. Windmill blades are made of oil and gas. The tower for a windmill has 100 tons of coal in it (the carbon component of steel). It is scientifically impossible to end the use of gas and oil and retain civilization.

The entire concept of green energy is a lie. Transitioning the United States off of gas and oil would result in famine and economic destruction that would leave the U.S. a third world country. The justifications for eliminating gas and oil are also lies. Climate change is a propaganda tool designed to bring about the political objectives of the global ruling class.

If the Climate Change movement succeeded in replacing every gas-powered vehicle with electric, our electric generation capacity would be able to power less than ten percent of them while still keeping the lights on in our homes and factories. When you factor in that they also want to shut down the natural gas and coal that produces 95 percent of our electricity, the entire concept falls apart and the real goal of the Climate Change agenda becomes clear.

The only possible outcome, and the ultimate goal of the climate change movement is for the elite to have electric cars and private jets while the rest of us hope for permission to take a train or other mass transit that is naturally, controlled by the ruling class. It's all about power, and not the kind that makes cars go. They do not intend to eliminate fossil fuel, they just want to control it, because they want to control us. Individual citizens, free to move about as they please, decrease the power of authority. Barriers, checkpoints and passes are the tools of authoritarians.

If our system were still free, thousands of entrepreneurs with thousands of alternatives would be competing for the attention of individuals who one at a time, making decisions in their own self-interest, would have replaced the 150-year-old gasoline combustion engine decades ago. Instead, the big three auto makers spent that time paying members of Congress to preserve their monopolies, prevent competition and stifle innovation.

The Climate Change movement is part of that system. In 2021 alone the U.S. government transferred two billion dollars from American workers to three multinational corporations for the production of electric cars. Anyone who has scientifically observed the efficacy of government spending can tell you that it will not likely result in more electric cars, but that wasn't the point. The point was two billion dollars, three large corporations, and no small businesses building any alternative.

The narrative that electric cars are necessary to save the planet is not the result of good scientific research. The process of mining, transporting, processing and eventually disposing of the rare earth metals, plastics and other materials required for electric cars has a greater negative impact on our environment than modern fossil fueled vehicles.

On February 7th, 1860 John Tyndall, an Irish scientist, in a lecture to the Royal Society in London warned that "a change in climate would harm humanity when too many heat trapping gases formed an atmospheric envelope on the temperature of the planet." 150 years later the planet was fine, but China had invested billions to destroy the United States and our energy revolution was foiling their plans. They had enough political influence to kill it, but they needed something more to convince the American people to go along.

Government subsidies for electric cars combined with penalties and tax deterrents for alternatives are leading the auto industry right where the China wants it. The Chinese Communist Party Inc. owns the mines that produce most of the worlds rare earth metals. They produce two thirds of the world's solar panels. They paid for the U.S. governments obsession with Climate Change. They finance studies into Climate Change, and everyone involved knows what results lead to future funding.

They are mandating that we haul hundreds of pounds of batteries around that need charged by a fossil fueled infrastructure made of millions of miles of copper wire strung through trees while viable alternatives like natural gas, hydrogen cells and E-gas are regulated out of business. Meanwhile China's building a new coal fired power plant every week. It obviously has nothing to do with the climate. The mandate, issued by executive order, instantly killed all financing for natural gas, hydrogen cells, E-gas and even an efficient steam engine made in Texas. It was paid for by the big auto producers. They can't go 100 percent electric and then have some small company come up with something better. The ruling class certainly doesn't want a viable e-gas or hydrogen vehicle on the market.

One of Joe Biden's first acts as President was to stop construction of the Keystone pipeline, preserving 40,000 eighteen wheeled tanker trucks that currently deliver oil from Canada and the Dakotas to Texas refineries. Those trucks will consume three quarters of a million tires, a billion gallons of diesel and several billion dollars' worth of road building and maintenance every year that the pipeline remains unfinished.

The people who stopped the pipeline are not trying to reduce carbon in the atmosphere. If they were, they wouldn't be paying a half million federal employees to drive to every address in the United States six days a week delivering thirty thousand trees worth of junk mail. If they had really wanted an electric vehicle infrastructure, they

45

would have put a charging station at every post office in the country. Killing the Keystone pipeline to damage the U.S. energy industry only makes sense if you are trying to weaken the United States as a world power. It is the opposite of what you would do if your goal was saving the planet.

A generation of Americans have been taught that the planet is in danger from kindergarten on. They have not been told that if the United States outlawed all fossil fuels tomorrow, or better yet if the United States was removed from the face of the Earth cows and all, in ten years it would reduce the increase of carbon in Earth's atmosphere by .02 percent.

In fact, according to the same scientific, mostly government reports that the Climate movement cherry-picked their evidence from, if the entire world's man-made carbon emissions were reduced to zero today, the planet would continue to warm for another 400 years. If man made carbon emissions continue on the current trajectory, the planet will continue to warm for another 400 years. Destroying U.S. economic superiority is a political goal and has nothing to do with the health of the planet.

The climate has been changing for four and a half billion years. For most of the time humans have walked the Earth it has been much colder than it is today. Historically speaking, the last ten or twelve thousand years have been unusually warm. All the advances in human civilization that we know of have taken place during this time.

The Climate movement has been remarkably consistent. Every prediction they've made for thirty years has failed to happen. Even if Al Gore had been right, the Climate Change movement's agenda would have done nothing to prevent "the entire North polarized cap" from disappearing in five years. What it *is* doing is bankrupting the United States and handing control of the world to China and the global ruling class.

The New Green Deal attracted a lot of attention for some of its goals, like eliminating cows and air travel, but the most outrageous part of the Deal attracted little attention. "Don't ask me how we're going to pay for it." The freshman Representative said. "This country is 23 trillion dollars in debt, and no one is asking how we're going to pay for that." Unfortunately, she was right, four years later the debt was 29 trillion. Our government is mathematically insolvent and no one in government is the slightest bit interested because federal spending is a monster with a life of its own. Our elected representatives are sucker fish along for the ride.

The ruling class fully intends to confiscate the proceeds of American production until the U.S. is reduced to something on par with the rest of the world so as to be less of an impediment to world government. A lot of people like Biden, Gore and Kerry are getting very wealthy along the way while a lot of working Americans are being forced out of business and out of work. Soon, we would be forced into line, asked for our papers (or chip) and sent to where the favored class has ordered us to be. Except that something unexpected happened.

Trump

It could have been anybody. Anybody outside of the system who also had the resources, name recognition and connections, and was willing to risk his wealth and family to challenge the hegemony of multinational corporations and global government agencies. In 2016 that narrowed the field to approximately one.

Donald Trump did not collude with Russians. He did not incite a mob to storm the Capitol. He did not lead an insurrection. He did something much worse. He threatened the ruling class. Everything that followed, from the Clinton/Steel Dossier to the installation of a demented crime family boss as President, was done in response to that threat.

As the government's debt grew beyond the ability of any tax rate to repay and government sponsored monopolies abused their increasingly powerless customers, official explanations became more contradictory and ludicrous. Brute force replaced accountability, propaganda served as truth, and it became harder to keep up the facade of a legal republic. They had convinced most Americans that most Americans believed the official explanations, but it was still mostly a media phenomenon. In homes, on farms and in businesses, millions weren't willing to trade freedom for the promises of an elite ruling class.

All it took to give voice to those people was for someone from outside the system who had a big enough microphone to call bullshit. That it was a flawed and unpolished billionaire with an arrogant pride in his own success added insult to injury. The ruling class and their sanctioned media responded hysterically because Trump was the antithesis of their victim-oriented propaganda. Propaganda that predisposed millions of Americans, taught since grade school that nice was good and winning was bad, to oppose and in some cases, hate Donald Trump.

Four years of attack, scandal and impeachment later the 2020 election was approaching, and Trump was more popular than ever. When Hunter Biden's laptop surfaced with evidence of the Biden family's criminal activities, the ruling class and their deep state allies reacted by confirming their own existence.

When the New York Post published the story of Hunter's laptop, their social media accounts were closed. Fifty former intelligence officials and at least 14 major media outlets told us that the story was Russian disinformation. A Google search for Hunter Biden's laptop returned no information from the New York Post story, but it listed millions of hits confirming that the story was Russian disinformation. The ruling class couldn't have written a more conclusive confession.

The ruling class, confident in their ability to control the narrative and re-write history, engineered the Presidency of a criminally compromised dementia patient and ordered all information outlets to discount or ignore evidence of Biden family corruption and election fraud.

Anyone who refused whether it was the highest rated show on cable news or a truck driver with a twitter account was silenced. So complete was the control of information that many average Americans stayed quiet out of fear as government officials supported rioters and ordered police to stand down as small businesses were burned and looted. The laptop disappeared, Hunter got a book deal and an art show.

Trump had bypassed the system to get elected and then implemented policies that threatened the ruling class and their global ambitions. He is lucky he just lost a rigged election because they were perfectly capable of taking him down the way they had Kennedy or Nixon.

Thousands of multi-national corporations and foreign governments use lobbying firms, campaign donations and business deals hidden behind shell companies and foundations that turn politicians into multi-millionaires who funnel billions to the multi-nationals who then insert their own wish lists into feet thick, trillion-dollar laws that no one reads.

Big banks get bailouts while paying hundred-million-dollar bonuses to their executives. We fight wars for big oil profits. Auto makers write regulations designed to squash competition from smaller companies. Nationwide minimum wage laws are written by big business in big cities to close small business in rural America.

Fighting this system pitted Trump against an entire world of financial, corporate and political elite. America First was great for the

American people but it would deprive the ruling class of the trillions of dollars they are stealing from American workers. They fought to destroy Trump for four years until the 2020 election raised the stakes. Trump was no longer just a threat to their profits; he threatened their existence. Had the election been allowed to proceed, crimes would have been exposed.

When Trump won, Hunter Biden's laptop, and the witnesses who were coming forward to corroborate it, would have exposed more than just the Biden family's corruption, it would have exposed the entire ruling class. Treason is an acceptable way of doing business in the U.S. government and very few of its representatives would have survived an honest investigation into where their money comes from.

After 37 years in the Senate earning $174,000 or less per year, Mitch McConnell admits to a net worth of over 34 million dollars, and he's been conservative in his extracurricular dealings. A lot of these people would have had a much harder time than Mitch explaining their fortunes. Trump's re-election had to be stopped at all costs and everyone in Washington was on board.

They weaponized a pandemic that didn't show up at just the right time by happenstance, to attack Trump and destroy his economy. They used it to justify mass mail-in voting and big city Democrats who had been rigging elections for decades introduced Venezuela style voting machines in at least six key states. By election eve they were confident in the outcome.

By the time the sun set on election day, they knew they were in trouble.

Multiple investigations determined that Dominion voting machines had programmable algorithms designed to allow vote totals to be adjusted by a preset percentage. After vastly underestimating how much adjustment would be needed to ensure a Biden victory, deep state operatives collaborated to stop the count in five states simultaneously. Overnight they brought in hundreds of thousands of fraudulent ballots to make up the difference. Dozens of counties in Arizona, Michigan, Wisconsin, Georgia and Pennsylvania counted more votes that night than they had voters.

What happened next was the greatest censorship campaign and cover-up in history. The period between November 5th and inauguration day was the most dangerous part of their scheme. They had stolen the election but were still in the getaway car.

A Google search after November 4th for election fraud returned 259,000,000 results, with not one mention of the substantial evidence of election fraud documented in these pages. Twitter banned Trump to stop him from revealing the evidence his team had collected. They shut down the accounts of his lawyers and team members who had worked to compile that proof as well as over 70,000 Americans who tweeted or re-tweeted the words "stop the steal".

Apple and Google removed Parler from their app stores and then Amazon shut down their servers because many of its 15 million users were disseminating unsanctioned information about the election. Every purveyor of information in the United States from Wikipedia to New York corporate media worked together to keep the mountain of evidence substantiating election fraud out of American discourse.

Radio stations and TV networks warned program hosts that perpetuating "the big lie" would not be tolerated. Members of Congress who had asked for an investigation into the election were accused of perpetuating "the big lie" and therefore contributing to insurrection.

Stating unequivocally that Joe Biden won the election legitimately became a litmus test for anyone wanting to work or do business in politics, publishing, television, radio or even distribute your private company's product to a national market. Entrepreneurs who supported Trump had their products banned from national retail outlets across the country.

This is not the behavior of people who think they are in the right. If they believed Biden won the election, they would have welcomed an investigation to put these allegations to rest. Instead, they banned speech. Labeling Trumps supporters' racists and domestic terrorists is no accident. It's what the Patriot Act was designed to do, to act against anyone who would challenge the ruling class. These are the actions of guilty people.

The fact that questions were not allowed, is by itself evidence.

Here is what is right in front of our faces. Millions of ballots were printed ahead of the election. Laws were changed, by judges and bureaucrats not state legislatures to allow these ballots to be counted regardless of where they came from, when they came in, whether they had a valid signature or whether they were cast by a U.S. citizen.

When polls closed on election night Trump was ahead in six key states. They stopped counting at around midnight and sent all of the poll watchers home. The next morning it was found that hundreds of thousands of votes had shown up over-night, behind locked doors, almost all for Joe Biden.

Trumps poll watchers were kept from seeing these ballots. Hundreds have signed affidavits swearing to have seen vans unloading ballots in the middle of the night, seen signatures on ballot after ballot in the same handwriting. But questions will not be tolerated.

During the four years that he was under attack, President Trump fought back by doing a good job for American people of every color. Wages went up and taxes went down. More Americans got better jobs than at any time in our history, especially blacks, Hispanics and women. He brought troops home and slowed illegal immigration. And he was the first President in 40 years to not start a war because he got elected without military-industrial money, which does include Apple, Google and Amazon.

One of the reasons Trump was such a threat was that he tended to keep his promises. One of those promises, school choice, would have freed hundreds of thousands of mostly black children stuck in under-performing government/union run schools. The ruling class and the wealthy already have school choice. They just oppose it for poor, black and working people. Those they need to control.

Freeing those people, offering them an escape from the gang and drug infested slums of government housing and welfare was a threat to the ruling class and their plans to bend the American people to the centralized will. Going forward, success will only come for the connected. Hard work only has value if you're free, it gains a slave little.

More Americans getting jobs was not what our rulers wanted. Fewer people on welfare were bad for the cause of world government. Middle- and upper-class black families threaten their hold on power. Controlling illegal immigration, workers keeping more of their own money and poor, mostly minority children choosing a better school were all bad for the people who run our country.

Rigged elections are and always have been the norm in this world. Our country was a rare exception.

History shows us that once a regime comes to power illegally, they can't allow dissent or opposition. Information about what happened in Detroit, Milwaukee, Atlanta and Philadelphia between election night and the morning of November 4, 2020, has been so thoroughly censored that talking about it is grounds for removal from public office and disqualification from current or future employment.

If you live in public housing, depend on the government to feed your family and your children are doomed to the same by their poorly run and violent school, you are where you belong. If you have started a small business or earn a good living in the energy industry, you are a problem to be corrected.

If you believe an illegal ruling class exists and is above the law, you will be silenced, many have been jailed, and it has only begun. They are stealing the wealth of our country on a scale that guarantees its collapse. Trump was either a failed last chance to save the United States, or the beginning of a movement that may yet save it.

Either way, it won't be easy, and it won't be peaceful. Our rulers have already shown that imprisoning political enemies, burning cities, killing cops and rigging elections is acceptable behavior if it furthers their cause and it's going to get much worse.

Trump is probably lucky they stole the election from us, and Joe Biden should be very afraid. The people who rigged the election would gain much if something happened to him now, especially if they could blame it on white supremacist domestic terrorism.

Trump intends to run again in 2024. They won't allow it. They made it clear that he would be arrested if he tried. If he and his family challenge the ruling class again, their lives and liberty will be at risk. The ruling authority was willing to sacrifice half of America's small businesses, several hundred thousand mostly elderly citizens and the integrity of our election system to get rid of him the first time. Their assassination teams are far more sophisticated than they were in the Dulles days. The official explanation of Trump's demise will be confirmed by a unified media, conspiracy theorists will be ridiculed and when a few vocal members of Congress demand answers, hearings will be held, committees formed, and investigations launched the results of which will be filed with the Mueller Report.

"Ideas are more powerful than guns. We would not let our enemies have guns, why should we let them have ideas." – Joseph Stalin

Covid

Masks are effective at keeping the bacteria in a surgeon or nurses mouth out of their patients' wounds during surgery or treatment. Anyone who prepares food for consumption by others should wear them. The human mouth is full of bacteria that is exhaled in water droplets that float in the air. Viruses are a million times smaller than bacteria. If someone across the room from you were to smoke a cigarette, when you smell the smoke, you are inhaling their viruses. Every time you take a breath you inhale trillions of them. Masks have no more effect on viruses than they do smoke. I learned these facts by taking on-line university courses in virology, SARS-CoV-2 and respiratory diseases. Everyone who has been to medical school knows or should know these facts. So why is everybody going along with the lie that masks prevent the spread of Covid? What else are they lying about?

People in power like having power and given the chance some will go to extremes to exercise it and even farther to keep power once they get it. Some people like being told what to do and when to do it, it's akin to being safe. These innate aspects of human nature act as a current that exerts constant pressure on our society towards authoritarianism. The ruling class understands this pressure and they used it to enhance the effect of the virus on our society. The only effective purpose masks and mask mandates have is making masses of people follow orders.

They want us to believe the pandemic was an isolated incident, a natural disaster, and that unquestioning obedience, censorship and shutting down small business is the only way to deal with it. While much of that story fell apart as information leaked out about the nature and origins of the virus, there is still no public information about the obvious connections between the pandemic and the rise of authoritarianism in America, or the motivation behind the cover-up and lies surrounding the virus.

We know that the Chinese Communist Party spent over fifty million dollars cultivating access to U.S. news outlets in the years leading up to 2020. We know that the U.S. government has a cozy relationship with corporate media. Misinformation has been used as a weapon in every war ever fought, but it's never been used as thoroughly and effectively as it was against the American people during the pandemic. Even referring to the virus as Chinese was roundly criticized. When Trump referred to it as a "foreign virus" the sanctioned USA Today called it "Racial discrimination and Xenophobia" saying the comment "goes against universal values of morality and humanitarianism" It was blatant propaganda designed to cover up the origin of the virus and encourage the population to submit to authority.

The George W. Bush administration shifted more power from the American people to their government than any President in history. The Obama administration joined more global initiatives and funded more alliances with World Government agencies than any President in history. The Biden administration's stated agenda came word for word from published World Government propaganda. The slogan "Build Back Better" was used by the U.N. to promote a plan to incorporate green energy goals into disaster relief. In July of 2020, the World Economic Forum released a white paper called Building Back Better outlining its guidelines for green building, sustainable transport, organic farming, urban open space, renewable energy and electric vehicles as part of its Utopian vision for the world in which *"we must all live sustainable lives, with equity and equality in all aspects of life,"* and that as a result, *"life will be much better for all."*

For world government to succeed, the United States must cede its sovereignty and that's what these men were doing, but they needed a world crisis or two to justify sacrificing the American people's freedom to a greater cause, so they created a climate crisis that would suppress energy production and lead to a global economic crisis. Before the plan could succeed the U.S. energy industry found vast reserves of oil and gas, then Donald Trump came along and threatened all their plans. They needed a new, more urgent global crisis and one agency of the World Government just happened to have one setting on a shelf.

The World Health Organization declared their operations off limits to oversight by any government or the public in 2009, the same time they began collaborating with pharmaceutical industry executives and virology research groups in the U.S. and China. A year or so after the pandemic we learned that the U.S. government, the pharmaceutical industry, World Health Organization and Chinese Communist Party worked together to hide the initial spread of Covid, cover up its Chinese bio-weapon origins and with the cooperation of Big Tech and corporate media, withhold information on therapeutics like Remdesivir, Hydroxychloroquine and zinc that could have saved countless lives, because effective treatments would have interfered with their plan to shut down the U.S. free enterprise economy which was still the largest single obstacle to world government.

The pharmaceutical industry and the cause of world socialism had a lot to gain, politically and financially from the pandemic. They also have a history of working together and experimenting on humans. During World War II, the Bank for International Settlements financed the construction and operation of factories in German concentration camps where hundreds of thousands of Jewish prisoners were exposed to experimental drugs while being worked to death. After the war, the guards at these factories were tried and executed by the Nuremberg tribunals. The bankers and executives went on to form multinational corporations. The largest factory at the Auschwitz concentration complex was reborn as the Bayer Corporation, one of the world's largest pharmaceutical companies and part of the World Health Organization's advisory board, and BASF, the world's largest chemical manufacturer. Both companies continued to work in the biological weapons field and were awarded billions in defense contracts by the U.S. government.

After the war, the CIA recruited Nazi scientists and overtly continued the German's experiments into the late 1960's when the project went off the books. In the 1970's, the U.S. Navy used a facility at Fort Detrick, the Center for Biological Warfare Research, later renamed the Fredrick Cancer Research Center, to develop cancer causing viruses. One of the viruses they isolated was called HTLV (Human T-cell Leukemia Virus) to which no human immunity exists. In a 1986 report to Congress the U.S. military admitted that they possessed biological agents including modified viruses, naturally occurring toxins, and agents that had been altered through genetic engineering. In 1994 a doctor at the MD Anderson Cancer Center in Houston named Garth Nicolson disclosed that many returning Desert Storm veterans were infected with an altered strain of Mycoplasma incognitus, a microbe commonly used in the production of biological weapons. Incorporated into its molecular structure is 40 percent of the HIV protein coat, indicating that it had been man-made.

The World Health Organization hid the origins of Covid. The U.S. scientific community covered it up, so did the U.S. sanctioned media. NBC, CBS, ABC, CNN, Facebook, Twitter and Google were all taking orders from the same people. So was the U.S. government. The Chinese led ruling class is in charge. The only ones lagging behind were some of the American people who thought they were still free. Now we are domestic terrorists.

Two years after the virus was released, the facilities and documents related to the research that had been done at the Wuhan lab were still off limits to investigators and journalists. The U.S. government still refused to release records of its gain of function research and Congress refused to investigate the origins of Covid. Social media still banned information about the viruses' origins or who may have paid for it. They were still covering up, because after everything that had come out, there was much more that they didn't want us to know.

Covid-19 was developed in cooperation with labs in the U.S. and other countries including China. One of many strains under development, Covid-19 was benign compared to many of the viruses they have developed. The common characteristic of these viruses is rapid human to human transmission. Covid mutated very slowly after billions of replications because it had been genetically modified to serve a specific purpose. The "variants" that appeared in the years following Covid-19 aren't random mutations of the original virus, they're off the shelf contingencies. As is the case in most crimes, the hard evidence is controlled by the perpetrators, but the circumstantial evidence is substantial.

We know that dozens of highly trained virologists in cooperation with hundreds of bureaucrats controlling billions of dollars collaborated to modify the genes of a virus known to be easily adapted to humans. It is reasonable to assume that they were not wasting their time, that the resulting virus had the characteristics they desired. Those characteristics were to rapidly spread through a population, bypass healthy individuals under the age of 65, and to be fatal for individuals over 65 or with health issues. Since we know it was created in a lab, it's reasonable to ask. Who had the most to gain from a pandemic with these characteristics? Who had the resources, opportunity and motive? And who lied about what they knew?

The Chinese Communist Party, World Health Organization and U.S. Government knew when the outbreak began that the virus was human engineered and that it originated in the Wuhan lab. The Chinese, W.H.O. and the U.S. government lied about its source, how it was spread and who and how many it was killing. They lied about these things because they had something to hide. There was no other reason to lie, and taken in the context of their previous behavior, it is incumbent on us to consider the possibility that the pandemic was not an accident.

The United Nations Biological Weapons Convention meets every four years. At the 2011 conference, scientists from the Wuhan lab reported on their work modifying genetic specific viruses to affect humans by race, age, health and other criteria. Four years later they reported nothing of interest and had no record of the previous reports.

The U.S. government knew in 2018 that the lab in Wuhan China was enhancing corona viruses. Federally funded labs in the U.S. sent enhanced corona virus samples to the Wuhan lab at the direction of the CDC. This lab, controlled by a military in enemy territory, received U.S. taxpayer funds authorized by the National Institute of Allergy and Infectious Diseases.

Gain of function research has no medical justification. It is bio-weapon research primarily aimed at theoretical social engineering. The fact that its release from the Wuhan lab was an accident, does not change the fact that it was designed for use on human populations. It was up someone's sleeve; it's use unthinkable until trillions of dollars were at stake and there were no other options.

When the existence of Covid-19 was first reported, there was a lot of readily available evidence that suggested the virus had been in the United States since late October or November of 2019. This included two university studies in California that revealed a high percentage of those tested already had Covid antibodies at the time of the studies in March of 2020. I have first-hand knowledge of individuals in Arkansas experiencing Covid- like symptoms in November of 2019 who later tested positive for Covid antibodies. By June, every mention of this evidence had been scrubbed from Google, Twitter, Facebook and sanctioned media.

The virus escaped from Wuhan China in December of 2019. While the Chinese Communist Party immediately isolated Wuhan from the rest of mainland China, flights into and out of the Wuhan International Airport continued unabated for the rest of the world, and since it had been involved from the beginning, the U.S. government had to know what was happening. If the virus had already been in the United States for at least two months, it's accidental release from the Wuhan Lab in December was a problem.

The prior existence of the virus in the U.S. had to be covered up until it could be explained in light of the accidental release in Wuhan. Thus, the unrestricted airport with hundreds of flights carrying thousands of Chinese into the United States, a W.H.O. issued statement in January saying that there was no danger of human-to-human transmission and a W.H.O. investigation concluding that the virus came from a farmers' market. We also had every information outlet in the United States parroting "indisputable evidence" that the virus could not have originated in a lab.

One of the ruling class's greatest coups was to be the takeover of the American health care system. It would put an additional 3 or 4 trillion dollars annually under their control and move a huge segment of the economy out of the private sector. But they had a problem. A relatively small, but growing demographic was using the lion's share of health resources and were no longer working and therefor weren't paying much into the system. The working theory as articulated by President Obama was for people over eighty to be given a pill and sent home.

The power of the ruling class is directly at odds with our individual freedom. For decades they were content to chip away at our liberties, until Trump came along and challenged their power. None of us, including Trump anticipated how hard they would fight to defend it. To what lengths would a criminal enterprise who's multi-trillion-dollar business was at risk not go? Trump's assault on the American Deep State and the global ruling class was enough to turn the unthinkable into a plan to not only stop Trump, but crush millions of independent businesses who don't contribute to Washington politicians in favor of giant multi-nationals who do.

Like U.S. immigration policy, Covid-19 was designed to change the demographic of the United States, to kill old and sick people for political purposes. Older Americans generally have more money than the rest of the population, consume more health care, pay fewer taxes and vote more conservatively. It was likely one of many contingencies and may have never been used if Trump hadn't forced their hand.

The average life expectancy in the United States in 2019 was 77. The median age of Covid victims in the United States was 78, many of whom could have been protected if our government and its sanctioned media would have told the truth instead of using the virus as a tool to harm Trump and his working class and small business voters.

Donald Trump had just spent three years attacking the Chinese Communist Party. He stopped funding for the World Health Organization, stopped illegal immigration and challenged the power of the U.S. ruling class. Then a virus shows up designed to further the agendas of the Chinese Communist Party, World Health Organization, the U.S. ruling class and as a bonus, destroy the greatest economy in history just in time for the election. The pandemic fits into the pattern of previous events orchestrated by the ruling class. Given the stakes, it would be naive to assume it was an accident.

The C.I.A.'s interest in population and demographic control may have been stimulated by another research project. In the 1990's when it became clear that we would eventually have a complete map of the human genome, American disease Associations lined up to be first in line for a cure for their cause, and the C.I.A. began to investigate solutions to the population and demographic catastrophe that would arise should these cures actually come to pass.

They pursued two parallel lines of investigation. The first monitored genetic research into diseases with a focus on classifying any disruptively rapid advances. The second funded and monitored research into designer pathogens that might moderate societal disruption caused by a sudden increase in life expectancy.

The projects generated several reports, all still classified. The first, issued in 1994, urged the U.S. and other governments to gain control of the worlds health care system in advance of any possible disruption. Subsequent reports called for mandatory health insurance tied to tax collection, the mass collection of data on citizens and centralized management of the world's population.

During the height of the pandemic, high ranking government officials were repeatedly caught ignoring the rules they claimed were vital for the rest of us. They weren't just being reckless; they knew something they were not telling the public. If the virus was created in a lab, which was no longer in doubt by July of 2021, it had a purpose and the ruling class were either aware that it was not as deadly as advertised, or they knew that its creators would have developed a vaccine for themselves, their families and their bosses before it was used on the public.

Federal and state governments crushed the economy with lockdowns, then offered the solution of vast stimulus measures that would destroy financial stability and fuel inflation. The pandemic was more excuse than justification. The virus did extraordinarily little to hurt actual business in the U.S. It was the lockdowns that did most of the damage. They did not spend trillions in stimulus to save employers and their workers, they did it to steal from them. They spent over eight trillion dollars in fourteen months with no mention of or care for whose money it was.

The lockdowns had no effect on the spread of the virus, but they did permanently kill almost half of all small businesses in the United States. How many independent restaurants were closed during the pandemic? Almost all of them. How many chain restaurants stayed open? Almost all of them. The resulting political and economic ramifications will kill far more people than the virus would have, but it will make a lot of rich and powerful people a whole lot more rich and powerful.

Trump had few options. If he hadn't gone along with the shutdowns, he would have been crucified with pictures of body bags lining the streets of cities across the country. He could have come out with the truth as soon as he suspected the true origin of the virus and the lies that came with it, but with sanctioned media, the Deep State and big tech aligned with the ruling class, the truth didn't stand a chance.

America wasn't supposed to have a state-run media, but it is obvious which side the New York corporate media monopoly was on. The few voices that questioned the wisdom of allowing power hungry mayors and governors to cause another great depression with ineffective shutdowns were either taken off the air or mysteriously quit asking unauthorized questions, at least until after the election.

New York City is the headquarters of sanctioned media. It's literately crawling with reporters, but not one of them noticed that all the 78-year-old people who usually die of old age each year, all died of Covid in 2020. Or that while the thousand bed hospital ship Comfort had almost no patients, infected elderly patients were placed into petri-dish nursing homes with people who were actually in danger from (or targeted by) the virus.

Covid-19 was developed as a population/health care management tool. It was deployed because too many older people voted for Trump, and it was not a top-secret plan known only to a few at the top. A large part of the socialist bureaucracy knew exactly what was going on. That's why Governors like Cumo and Whitmer let Covid facilities lie empty while putting elderly victims back in nursing homes to infect the rest of the elderly population. The last thing they wanted was anything that might improve the situation. They needed a national emergency. The Constitution had to be suspended. This was a modern-day Holocaust committed because Donald Trump threatened the ruling class.

A free enterprise economy is a living, breathing thing. You can't turn it off and expect to wake it up again. Businesses lost employees, customers, and vendors. Inventories became obsolete. Methods, procedures and talents were lost. The interdependent connections between thousands of small companies and millions of people disintegrated, and trillions of dollars conjured out of nothing distorted the economic foundations of property and ownership. Half of America's small business will never return.

The death rate from Coronavirus was minuscule compared to the death rate from every-day life in countries outside of the U.S. and its free enterprise influence. Entrepreneurship and small business are features of a free society. They undermine socialist systems which have always tried to eliminate them. The United States has suffered a massive and permanent shift of money and power from individuals and small business to multinational corporations and from representative government to a China led world government.

Our rulers know they can't keep spending an amount equal to the entire output of the country every eight months without crashing the system, but they can delay the crash by increasing production (working people) and decreasing expenses (old people). It is hard to believe they would kill millions of Americans for 15 or 20 trillion dollars, only because their control of information is so thorough that most people don't realize that the ruling class has behaved this way for decades. Once you get away with killing a President, then killing his brother because he dared to run for President, this bit of murder probably came easy.

Tyranny is more dangerous than Covid.

"One of the saddest lessons of history is this: If we've been bamboozled long enough, we tend to reject any evidence of the bamboozle. We're no longer interested in finding out the truth. The

bamboozle has captured us. It's simply too painful to acknowledge, even to ourselves, that we've been taken. Once you give a charlatan power over you, you almost never get it back" Carl Sagan

2020 Election

The statement "*there is no evidence of fraud in the 2020 presidential election*" has been debunked.

The 2020 election ranks with the 16th Amendment, the Federal Reserve and the Great Depression as one of the most heinous crimes committed against the American people by this country's ruling class. Facebook, Twitter and the state sanctioned media confirmed that the evidence existed when they banned it from their broadcasts and social media pages. They openly censored true stories and promoted stories they knew to be false in support their side of the political divide. They have no respect for, or fear of mere citizens because their side has judges and prisons.

The Justice Department spied on Trump's 2016 campaign using evidence manufactured by the Clinton campaign. During the 2020 campaign big tech and sanctioned media worked with federal law enforcement to run a full-blown censorship campaign on Hunter Biden's laptop. The New York Post was banned for reporting true information. Election fraud is not new in America, but it was only effective in close elections. Our country was too free, our elections too transparent and our press too diligent for an outright coup. That all changed in 2020.

Donald Trump won a landslide victory with 13 million more votes than he received in 2016. When the four critical swing states went dark at midnight, everyone knew what was going down. Everyone knows Trump won. Joe Biden knows. That's why they staged a phony insurrection and locked down the Capital. That's why over 600 of the million or so voters that showed up in Washington to protest the rigged election were imprisoned. Nearly 80 million voters were labeled domestic terrorists by the D.H.S. Domestic Security Police.

On Monday, December 21, 2020, Michigan's 13th Circuit Judge Kevin Elsenheimer released the results of a court ordered audit of Dominion voting machines. The audit concluded that the Dominion Voting System is intentionally and purposefully designed with inherent errors to create systemic fraud and influence election results.

The report also found that there were attempts to "tamper with evidence." Analysis revealed that on November 21, an "unauthorized user unsuccessfully attempted to zero out election results". The report also found that all security logs from Election Day, and the days prior to and after November 3, had vanished. The report was banned from newspapers, broadcast news and social media.

Hundreds of witnesses documented under oath that fraudulent ballots were trucked, delivered and counted in the hours between midnight and 7:00 AM November 4th. By morning all witnesses had been threatened and intimidated into silenced and the results of the election were censored, but enough information had already become part of the public record to discern the truth.

At midnight on Election Night, according to the Associated Press and Edison/Decision Desk, President Trump had a lead of 112,022 votes in Wisconsin, 293,052 votes in Michigan, 356,945 votes in Georgia and a lead of 555,189 votes in Pennsylvania. A short time later precincts in Detroit, Milwaukee, Atlanta and Philadelphia stopped counting, locked the doors and sent election officials home.

Updates to the election totals after election officials were sent home and before the sun came up on November 4th were more than extraordinarily anomalous, they were statistically impossible. Here are four examples taken from information published by the New York Times after the election.

An update in Georgia at 1:34 AM Eastern Time on November 4th, shows 136,155 votes for Joe Biden and 29,115 votes for Donald Trump

An update in Wisconsin at 3:42 AM Central Time on November 4th, shows 143,379 votes for Joe Biden and 25,163 votes for Donald Trump

An update in Michigan at 3:50 AM Eastern Time on November 4th, shows 54,497 votes for Joe Biden and 4,718 votes for Donald Trump

An update in Michigan at 6:31 AM Eastern Time on November 4th, 2020, shows 141,258 votes for Joe Biden and 5,968 votes for Donald Trump

The 3:42 AM update in Wisconsin alone erased a Trump lead of more than 100,000 votes and put Biden in the lead. Those votes have since disappeared and are not available for examination or recount.

The 1:34 AM spike in Georgia came less than three hours after surveillance video showed cases of votes pulled from a hidden space under a covered table, again after election officials were sent home. These votes have also not been made available for examination.

The rate of mail-in ballots rejected for errors in Georgia was 6.4% in 2016, 3.1% in 2018, and 0.6% in 2020 when there were many more mail-in ballots. The discrepancy represents hundreds of thousands of improperly cast ballots that should not have been counted. Biden won votes placed in drop boxes in Georgia by a 5 to 1 margin. Drop boxes were illegal under Georgia law.

If not for extremely anomalous updates posted in the middle of the night and behind closed doors, Joe Biden would have lost the states of Michigan, Wisconsin, and Georgia, giving him 42 fewer Electoral votes and putting him below the number required to win the Presidency.

The evidence is overwhelming, but Common Sense is enough to tell us who won the 2020 election.

In the days before the election tens of thousands of Americans showed up at three and four Trump Rallies per day and we're supposed to believe he lost to an elderly dementia patient who couldn't draw flies to his rallies.

More than twice as many blacks voted for Trump in 2020 than in 2016.

At least 40% more Hispanics voted for Trump in 2020 than in 2016.

Trump got 13 million more votes in 2020 than in 2016.

Of the two million plus people who attended a Trump rally in 2019 and 2020, 25 percent of them were Democrats.

At least 75 million registered voters with an ID, a signature and an address voted for Trump. Vastly more than any candidate in history.

In 2020 alone, 17 million Americans purchased a weapon, most for the first time. But we are supposed to believe that they voted for Biden/Harris who have pledged to take them away.

In Nevada on Dec. 16 attorney Jesse Binnall testified before the Senate Homeland Security Committee. He had proof of nearly 90,000 fraudulent or improper votes that were cast, including instances where:

More than 42,000 people voted multiple times.
At least 1,500 people listed as "dead" voted.
More than 19,000 non-residents voted.
In excess of 8,000 people cast mail-in votes from non-existent addresses.
Over 15,000 votes were cast from commercial or vacant addresses.
Nearly 4,000 non-citizens voted.

Biden took Nevada by 33,596 votes.

In Pennsylvania a group of 17 Republican state lawmakers released a statement alleging 202,377 more votes were cast than there were voters who voted. State Rep. Frank Ryan, who has a background as a certified public accountant, led the investigation and released a statement.

"These numbers just don't add up, and the alleged certification of Pennsylvania's presidential election results was absolutely premature, unconfirmed, and in error,"

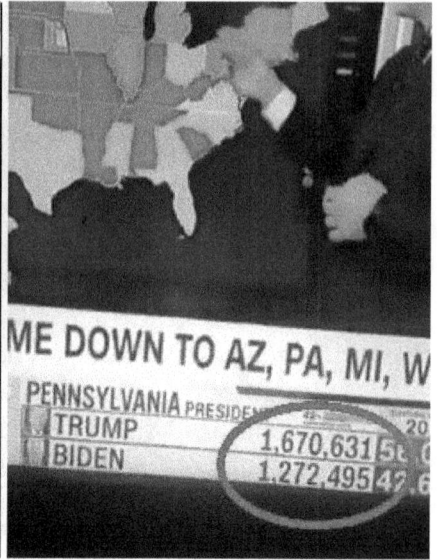

Already counted Trump Votes disappeared on live television.

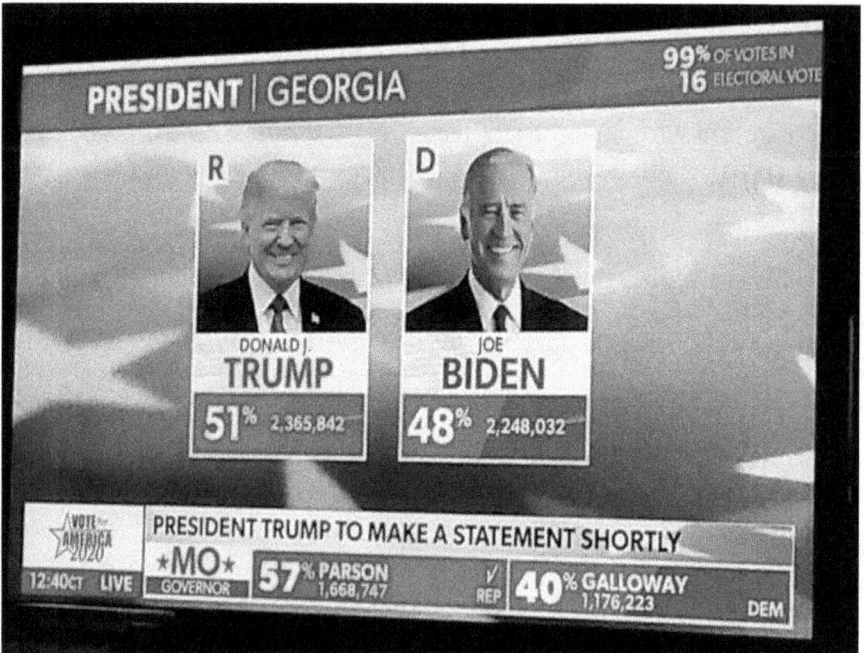

At 1:40AM with 99% of all votes in, President Trump had a 117,000-vote lead, or, 3%. in Georgia.

On December 17, 2020, Peter Navarro released a report on the 2020 Election, "The Immaculate Deception: Six Key Dimensions of Election Irregularities." The following was taken directly from "The Navarro Report".

Georgia	Pennsylvania	Michigan	Wisconsin
Trump Lead at Midnight 11/3			
356,945	555,189	293,052	112,022
Biden "Lead" 12/15			
11,779	81,660	154,188	20,682

Table S: Summary: 2020 Presidential Election Results and Fraud

State	Electoral Votes	Vote Margin	Fraudulent Votes
Pennsylvania	20	81,660	747,000
Georgia	16	11,779	425,000
Michigan	16	154,188	456,000
Arizona	11	10,457	224,000
Wisconsin	10	20,682	348,000
Nevada	6	33,596	145,000

Full Report:

The 2020 Presidential election was so compromised that an unelected team occupies the White House. It is the biggest story since Kennedy's assassination. No news outlet has covered it.

Joe Biden

Joe Biden will be an unlikely, but significant figure in the history of the United States as he will likely be the man who presides over its final collapse.

He went to Washington when many politicians still leaned towards defending the Constitution and the freedom of U.S. citizens. Joe did his share in that fight, but there was also an element that sold deals under the table, and that's where Joe found the real source of power in government. Fifty years later he was openly selling influence to foreign governments, corporations and others. His corruption was exposed to federal authorities and the national media, both of whom covered it up.

Hunter Biden was paid 5 million dollars by the Chinese oil company CEFC. He started a one-billion-dollar investment fund with the state-owned bank of China. Received a 3.5-million-dollar wire transfer from Elana Baterina, the wife of the former mayor of Moscow. And earned 83 thousand dollars per month to serve on the board of Burisma, a Ukrainian energy company. All while Joe was Vice President.

When Hunters laptop exposed the extent of the corruption and Joe's involvement, the evidence was censored and more than fifty former intelligence community officials including five former CIA directors signed a letter attesting that the laptop was a Russian plot. At the same time, the Justice Department was sending storm troopers into the homes and offices of Trump associates. At the end of his career, with signs of dementia obvious to those around him, Biden was installed at the top of a puppet government after what even the Biden administration knows was the most corrupt election in U.S. history.

They created a superficially convincing illusion. If you watch television or read Twitter you would think that Joe Biden was the legitimate President of the United States, but the people who engineered the Biden Presidency did not have the consent of the people and their actions show that they knew it. The Capital was immediately occupied by an armed force and surrounded with Razor wire. The so called "Biden Administration" then advanced an aggressive Marxist agenda largely dictated from the offices of the Chinese Communist Party. No elected President would have attempted or could have gotten away with this kind of open and obvious treason.

Using a record number of executive orders and extremely partisan legislation passed using quasi-legal political maneuvers and propaganda, they consolidated power, rewarded allies and punished opponents. No election will ever remove them because no one elected them in the first place. Most of the Deep State agenda that without Trump's disruption would have played out over the next twenty years or so, was rushed into place in a couple of years.

They did not even try to appease the 75 or 80 million Americans who voted for lower taxes, less regulation, American energy and legal immigration. The new political argument was that Trump's voters were domestic terrorists and there was no room for their voice in the public square and no place for their representatives in the halls of power.

It's obvious that the Biden administration doesn't believe in its own legitimacy. Anyone who doubts its legitimacy is part of the greatest threat facing our country today. The January 6 "insurrection" was worse than the Civil War. Disagreeing with the administration is an attack on "democracy". Anyone who protested the rigged election were domestic terrorist trying to overthrow the government.

Like illegitimate regimes everywhere, they censor information, imprison political enemies and fabricate disinformation. They don't even pretend to be constrained by the consent of the governed, most of whom it treats as enemy combatants. They operate reeducation camps in our schools, where the next generations are brainwashed into hating America and advocating that it must be replaced by the regime. Unelected bureaucrats in our military and intelligence agencies police dissent against the regime.

They nationalized private property, ordering property owners to allow people to live in their houses rent free. When the Supreme Court ruled it to be unconstitutional, the CDC director ordered it to continue anyway. They threw open our borders in violation of the wishes of our country's citizens and its laws. The American people are no longer sovereign. We have no control of our property, our borders or our elections. Our country has been stolen from us. It is treason.

Only insurrectionist's worry about voter fraud. The 2020 election was fair, and Biden is not a crook installed in the White House in a ruthless coup. If a family member or neighbor says different, you should turn them in to the authorities. The leader of the opposition has been banned from social and most broadcast media, civil liberties are suspended, and private property confiscated. If you dare to collect rent from people living on your property, you will be jailed along with the conspiracy theorists, insurrectionists and white supremacists. The unvaccinated have been excluded from the workforce, stores and public/government transportation, all of which have electronic surveillance by the way.

Tyrants who do not have the consent of the people, must have eyes and ears everywhere. They must stomp out all hints of opposition. The Biden administration's proposed 3.2 trillion-dollar infrastructure bill contained a law requiring all new cars be equipped with an electronic surveillance device. The bipartisan 1.2 trillion-dollar infrastructure bill eliminated subsidies for trans-gender owned businesses but kept the surveillance requirement. In 2021 Department of Transportation officials are confiscating vehicles that don't comply with certain environmental laws. So far, they're mostly looking for diesel vehicles that have had the device removed that disables it when you don't buy diesel exhaust fluid. How long before they look for your surveillance device?

Joe Biden was a pawn in a much larger game. He is insignificant to the story of America's fall. The government of the United States is financially insolvent, and the world's interconnected economy is balanced on a less than convincing lie. Its collapse is imminent and inevitable.

Insurrection

Angry protesters marched and shouted their way through the marbled buildings of Capitol Hill and even blocked a Senate elevator door to confront Senator Jeff Flake on live TV. But that was not an insurrection, it was liberals storming the Capital during 2018 hearings on Brett Kavanaugh's Supreme Court appointment.

The January 6th, 2021, attack on Capitol Hill by thousands of deranged MAGA hat wearing insurrectionists was a seminal event in American history. It exposed the true nature of corporate-government complex that controls this country.

After the real insurrection on election night in 2020, political dissent could not be allowed. It was obvious from the start that the narrative about what happened at the Capital January 6th was an orchestrated lie, but the truth was not clear. After millions of Trump supporters attended three and four rallies a day for months with no violence, not even leaving trash behind, it didn't make sense that the same people became violent insurrectionists.

Many suspected BLM or some other liberal instigators were behind the "attack". Months later we learned the truth. More than five hundred political protesters were arrested and jailed on trumped up charges. The arrest reports reveal that about twenty individuals who instigated the attack were not arrested, because they were undercover agents of the U.S. Justice Department, mostly FBI. Now we know why fourteen thousand hours of video recorded that day has been hidden, probably destroyed or at least adulterated.

In 2016 Donald Trump threw a monkey wrench into the ongoing, and damn near complete overthrow of representative government in the United States. The real surprise is that he managed to continue as long as he did.

The looting, burning and murdering in cities across the U.S. during 2020 that destroyed two billion dollars' worth of property and cost dozens of innocent lives were *"mostly peaceful protests"* because they were mostly burning private property. The Capital Hill protest targeted our rulers in their castle and that was treasonous.

Private property is a measure of freedom. It is the direct result of true representative government. From now on wealth will be distributed to the masses by those in power. Unequal outcomes among the general population will not be tolerated.

When a hedge-fund forces a stock to zero, so they get to keep all the money, it's market forces. Individual investors gang up on social media and cost the hedge-fund billions, it's a hate crime. Trading is halted, social media accounts closed, and new laws passed to prevent future hate crimes. Covid was used to close small business while Home Depot, Verizon, hell, every name listed on the New York stock exchange, remained open for business. The people will learn who's in charge here.

The next election? Hell, if you supported the wrong guy in the last election your business was shut down, you were blacklisted from working for a major corporation and you have been labeled a domestic terrorist. There will never be another free election in this country.

The protesters in the Capitol on January 6th, 2021, were protesting a stolen election. The people who had just taken power illegally couldn't allow that. Anyone who accepted the invitation of undercover FBI agents and Capitol Hill police that day and entered the Capital were arrested within days. Over the next six- or eight-months people were arrested for committing no other crime than attending the Trump rally.

The illegal government was especially paranoid about resistance within their own institutions. Anyone who worked for the government or one of the large government sponsored corporations and attended the rally were fired and then arrested. Mark Abrahim was a DEA agent who committed no crime beyond attending the rally. He was fired, arrested and as of July 2021, faced fifteen years in federal prison for being part of a crowd that stood too close to a federal monument.

Only illegitimate governments behave this way. The "insurrection" was staged to head off any attempts to expose a rigged election. Almost everyone with any power at all in Congress had taken part in the corrupt business of selling influence. They all had much to lose if Trump got re-elected and actually drained the swamp enough to expose it.

Money is no object for the federal government because it's our money and they no longer need our permission to spend it. If you live in subsidized housing, send your kids to a government school, and collect food vouchers to feed your family, you're exactly where you belong. If you own a small business or have a good job, you are out of line. Policies have been implemented to correct the problem. If you supported President Trump, you are a threat. He won't be allowed to run in 2024, if he tries, he will be arrested or worse.

Trumps policies created more jobs and higher wages for every class of American, especially minorities. His next step, school choice would have freed millions of mostly minorities from the trap of government school-housing-welfare. The global elite could not allow that because free people can't be controlled. Trumps second impeachment, troops in the capital, the killing of Parler and banning of conservative speech were paranoid acts by people who knew they had stolen a U.S. Presidential election but weren't yet confident they had gotten away with it. Now that they have gotten away with it, they will take their place as pawns in a much larger game.

Racism

It is a fact. White people rule the world. Our 200-year-old techno-industrial civilization has existed for .003 percent of the time modern humans have lived on Earth. That it was created by white people is irrelevant. It could have just as easily been created by people of any color; it almost certainly has been. It happened this time where white people lived because that's where circumstances provided the challenges that inspired it. The fact that the guy who discovered electricity was white, is not racist. If you want to find the racist, find the guy who cares that he was white.

It is a fact, America was founded by white people, and America's founding promise that all men are created equal was the greatest barrier to racism and every other form of tyranny that man has ever devised. If you want to find the racist, find the guy who wants to tear that down.

Human's slaughter other humans, always have. Usually at the urging of their rulers. Slavery did not start in 1619 and the United States was not founded by racists. It was founded amid human cruelty because it was founded by humans. That it was not founded in the Garden of Eden is only useful to those who would destroy it.

There are bad people, but 98 percent of humans are not killers, not ignorant and we are not racist. We don't refuse to hire, serve or help someone because of what color they are. Systemic racism in the United States only exists as government policy. The ruling class uses it to keep the serfs in our place. The free market is colorblind. The one man whose policies created more jobs at higher wages for the poorest Americans of every color was run out of Washington because it threatened the people with private schools, private security and gated homes. It threatened the ruling class.

The promise that all men are created equal is a threat to those who want power over other humans. The thieves who are at the receiving end of our tax system orchestrate racial tensions, then offer to use the force of government to hurt others, people who are not like you. It feels like it helps you because your condition improved relative to others, but the only one it really helps is the ruling class. They have a lean on our labor. They mark us by the wholly irrelevant feature of skin color for the same reason the jail puts prisoners in matching orange jump suits, control.

Color doesn't matter, until you want to subjugate a civilization. Then color becomes very convenient. The ruling class has used its illegal taxing authority to spend trillions segregating Americans by color. For decades, the welfare state has targeted black and brown people, punishing them for raising their children in traditional families, disincentivizing work ethic and forcing children into substandard government schools. When the desired outcome was achieved, they blamed the other group of Americans, the ones who had jobs and owned buildings. Which led to the next desired outcome.

There is systemic racism in the United States and so far, blacks have been far more likely to be its victim. It is propagated by those in power for profit. It is perpetrated by big city teachers' unions who pay millions each year to politicians to prevent millions of mostly minority children from escaping the union's monopoly on incompetent education. The federal government's systematic racism has destroyed the structure of family in minority communities.

It is perpetrated by big city mayors and liberal governors whose primary income is federal dollars that are used to segregate their citizens and insulate them from market forces that would offer escape. It is perpetrated by multinational corporations that build business models around federal benefits programs while they locate factories in and buy their goods from other countries. It's perpetrated by the ruling class as a means of gaining power over other humans.

Our political and corporate leaders have school choice. They wouldn't consider sending their children to the government schools our children attend. The entrenched ruling class has a vested interest in preventing millions of poor Americans from escaping poverty. Their policies destroy families, promote dependency and trap people in poverty because it justifies billions of dollars each year that people in power take from working Americans of every color. They are destroying equal opportunity and individual, colorblind liberty.

The federal war on drugs, waged in direct violation of the constitutional limits placed on the federal government, set in motion a tough-on-crime policy that percolated through the justice system. Since 1971 the government has spent over a trillion dollars enforcing these laws for which black Americans are nearly six times more likely to be incarcerated than whites. It created an adversarial relationship between police and poorer black communities that served a purpose that had nothing to do with, or any effect on drug use. Like Climate Change and Covid, the war on drugs was a tool designed to increase the serfdom of its victims and the power of their rulers.

When Trump cut taxes and regulations, federal revenues increased, wages increase, and unemployment dropped among every ethnic group. In 2020 twice as many blacks and 40 percent more Hispanics voted for Trump than in 2016. Some Texas border counties, 95 percent Hispanic who voted 90 percent for Hillary shifted to Trump by 40 to 50 percent. It had to be stopped. The same politicians who supported the drug laws for fifty years accused Trump's voters of racism. It was so dangerous that razor wire went up, troops were called in to protect the Capital and Homeland Security shifted from Islamic Fundamentalists to White Domestic Terrorists.

Pepe Le Pew, Elmer Fudd and Speedy Gonzales are racist while cable and Saturday morning cartoons broadcast sick propaganda produced by the same multi-national corporation that indoctrinates Chinese children into the Communist Party. If you are one of the more than two million Americans who attended a Trump rally in 2020, you are a suspected racist even if you are black.

Freedom is dangerous for tyrants. Individuals are hard to control. Mobs are easy to control. The people in power need to keep poor and minority communities where they belong. They used their information monopoly to encourage their victims to burn their neighbors' businesses and attack their community's police. It is orchestrated by the ruling class to destroy private property. They need more poor people to be dependent on the state and they're getting them. Private property is a symptom of "all men are created equal". The people who run this country are doing everything in their power to stomp it out.

It is not an accident that the loudest social activist corporate entities in America are the ones with the largest markets in Communist China. You can't buy an inexpensive pair of shoes in America that are free of slave labor, but the corporate social conscience police will boycott a State or ban a political party while they sell them to you.

In 2021 the nations federal law enforcement openly declared war on a segment of the U.S. population they identified by skin color. Two Senators openly stated that they would not vote to confirm any Biden nominees who were the wrong color. These Senators are being used by the same people who are using our children when they are told that

America is racist while being taught how to get an EBT card but not how to read.

If you want 350 million people to live together peacefully, we must be treated as individuals. Those who want to exercise power over 300 million people, divide us into groups, and then convince us that we hate each other. Ruling class, or master? It's only a matter of time.

War on Drugs, People

When the U.S. government wanted to prohibit alcohol, they knew they needed to amend the Constitution to do it. By the 1930's Congress had decided that they were smarter than the dead guys who had written the Constitution so in 1937 they passed a law prohibiting marijuana. It would be more than eighty years before a Supreme Court justice would mention the fact that the law was illegal. As with the prohibition of alcohol 17 years earlier, the law forced the distribution of marijuana underground. The underground distribution network that emerged over the next few decades reached into practically every town and high school in the United States.

The statement that marijuana use leads to the use of harder drugs is true, but not because the plant is a gateway drug. It's because the underground network its prohibition created was used to distribute other substances that there would have never been a market for otherwise. The same guy you bought your pot from in high school can provide you with hashish, cocaine or heroin. More dangerous than the trillion-dollar underground drug trade is the culture of unconstitutional government overreach it represents.

It turns out that politicians are not smarter than this country's founders, and they are not smarter than you or me. The gist of the laws that are supposed to govern our country, the Constitution, is that no one is smarter than you or me when it comes to deciding what is right for you or me as long as it doesn't hurt anyone else. Unfortunately, Congress and the hundreds of thousands of bureaucrats they empower, are positive that without their oversight, we will all descend into drug addicted poverty. There is evidence for just the opposite.

The Constitution is very clear about what the federal government is allowed to do, and it very clearly states that all else is prohibited to it. When lawmakers ignore the rules and take matters into their own hands "because they are smarter than the people they govern" it always leads to disaster. The war on drugs has cost the American people over a trillion dollars. We spend 10 million dollars a day incarcerating people for using drugs. Result, more people die every year from drug overdoses.

There is a direct cause and effect line from the 1937 law prohibiting marijuana through the war on drugs to the more than 100,000 people who died in 2019 of drug overdoses because federal lawmakers are trying to do things, they lack the legal authority or proclivity to do. The States have the constitutional authority to prohibit any substance their people wish. Some States would have gotten it right, and the rest of us could either move there or change our state's laws accordingly.

That's how our system is supposed to work, but that system was replaced by a military/banking/information/industrial complex bent on global power who needed to control the nation, it's people and most importantly, it's money. In order to do that, they had to get around the Tenth Amendment. They really didn't care about pot, but the law was a gateway drug for all the unconstitutional laws that have come since.

Gun rights advocates have spent billions fighting to defend Second Amendment rights, but the Second Amendment wasn't the one that would have protected our right to bear arms. That would have been the Tenth Amendment. The successful nationwide prohibition of substances by the federal government, supported by most conservatives, was the first step in the plan to take our guns. Which they need to complete in order to take our property.

A brief history lesson will confirm what this nation's founders did their best to mitigate, governments are dangerous. The only thing standing between us, and tyranny are the few pages of plain language in our country's constitution. The government makes law that we must follow. The Constitution is the law that the government must follow. Each time we allow the government to violate its law, the foundations of citizen sovereignty are shaken, and the reverberations continue for generations.

Since 1971, the war on drugs has cost the United States over a trillion dollars. That money turned police departments across the country against the citizens they were meant to protect, cities burned, and politicians condoned and, in some cases, encouraged the destruction of private property.

War in the Streets

In 2020 when police tried to serve a drug warrant in Philadelphia, the suspect fired on the cops hitting six of them. During the shootout and ensuing standoff, residents taunted and threw rocks and cans at police. During the live coverage of the incident, reporters didn't understand why people were reacting to the police that way. By the next morning, all reference to the behavior of bystanders had evaporated.

Every evening we watch the news and see cops being targeted and citizens facing cops armed with military equipment. We've seen this kind of adversarial relationship between authority and citizens throughout history and around the world, in countries with authoritarian governments. It doesn't happen in a free country.

There are other things going on in our country that should not be happening in a free country. A hundred thousand citizens dead of drug overdose. Entire public-school systems in which not one student can pass a basic math, reading or writing test. The cost of higher education has skyrocketed while the value of a college degree borders on worthless. 40 million people don't have enough food, a million are homeless and a higher percentage of our population is in prison than any country on Earth.

All these problems have one thing in common, and one root cause. The federal government has taken responsibility away from individuals and local communities where it legally belongs. Police departments used to know the people they were there to protect. They were the husbands, wives, siblings and children of the communities they worked in. When the federal government started sending weapons, equipment and primarily money into police departments, they separated them from their communities. When the federal government took authority, it is prohibited from having, it became far more dangerous than any criminal.

The United States spends 51 billion dollars per year fighting drug abuse, 68 billion on education, about 50 billion on government housing and over 100 billion on food and food subsidies. All these problems have gotten worse in almost exact proportion to the amount spent by the federal government because most of the money ends up making the people in charge of it wealthier. The government needs more people on drugs, in bad schools, in government housing and standing in line for food because that is the source of their power over the people.

The harm that excess spending is doing to this country is far more insidious and closer to home than balance sheets and income statements. It's not incompetence. It is the deliberate theft of private property and destruction of our free society so that people in charge will have more power. It is the purposeful empowerment of an authoritarian ruling class.

Lawyers

The most effective system of government in history was simple. All its rules encompassed by a few pages, easily understood by every citizen. By 1960 the rules wouldn't fit in a shipping container. The mountain of rules created a demand for scholars of the rules called lawyers. Citizens were obliged to pay a scholar to find the rule they needed, to keep their land for example, but someone with more resources would find another scholar to find a better rule to take your land for his parking lot. If the rule you need doesn't exist, it can be written for a price, no one will notice a couple more pages in a mountain of paper. In 2021, somewhere in the neighborhood of half a million pages were added to the mountain.

I know lawyers who do good work. I had a mentor growing up who was a lawyer. He had a sign in his lobby that said, "Some small towns won't support a lawyer, but they'll all support two." Back then, I thought it was funny. Now, I know it's sad. The problem is not individual lawyers, it's the legal system's role in government.

The business of law bears not a little resemblance to the business of religion, except that the scripture lawyers interpret for the masses is far more voluminous than the Bible, and so is the expected contribution. The practice of law is the only business that entirely regulates and disciplines itself. Attorneys are the only professionals not protected by whistle blower laws. In fact, it can be a disbarable offense for an attorney to publicly criticize another attorney or judge, or for judges to criticize each other.

The mountain of paper has so obfuscated the rule of law that you can't start a business, rent a building or die without paying a lawyer. If a government bureaucrat decides he wants some of my property, my only recourse is to hire a lawyer, who will challenge the State's lawyer in front of another lawyer in a taller chair who will decide the State quoted better scripture. I can appeal the decision, to more lawyers, and when that doesn't work, I'll call my congressman, who is another lawyer.

The whole thing makes me so mad that I'm not paying attention and get run over by a truck. The lawyers decide the accident was my fault, but I can't go to work. When I can't pay my bills, people come to take my stuff, so I hire a lawyer who if I pay in advance, will file papers to hold off my creditors. He tells me about Social Security Disability. Great, I say. Where do I apply? You need a lawyer he says. It's a specialty. Law schools teach it, they graduate hundreds of lawyers every year who build practices that do nothing else. Hell, if you get one of these lawyers, you don't even need to be disabled.

In business there are good times and bad. Often during the tough times my customers would go out of business. In a typical case, a boat company filed on December 1, 2004. In April of 2009, over four years later, I was still receiving court documents authorizing payment of attorney's fees out of the company's assets. The Judge had appointed some lawyers to represent creditors in the case, and more lawyers to represent those lawyers in case they did something wrong. Eventually, all of the assets had been liquidated and the lawyers had been paid. The case was closed.

A few years later my company was named in a product liability lawsuit. The lawyer who filed the suit was working on a contingency basis. His client didn't pay, the lawyer would get paid only if he won. The suit was baseless, and everyone involved knew it, but the attorneys for my liability insurance carrier settled for attorney's fees because it was cheaper than fighting it. The plaintiff got nothing, my insurance rates went up, but the lawyers got paid. That's a specialty also. Law schools graduate hundreds of lawyers each year who go through their careers filing contingency suits and settling for attorney's fees. It's cooked into the mountain of paper.

The judicial branch of government was created to protect our rights as articulated by the constitution. In practice, its primary function is to generate attorney's fees. When it was discovered that asbestos caused cancer, a new legal specialty was born. They filed over a million lawsuits, bankrupted hundreds of companies and generated over a hundred billion dollars in attorney's fees, many times more than victims received.

Americans spend about $15,000 each on health care. Less than half of that pays for actual heath care, the rest is the cost of dealing with the rules, largely related to liability, all involving lawyers. In a nation governed by lawyers, liability follows the money. If you are injured riding a defective skateboard and the skateboard manufacturer has no money, the liability goes to the owner of the parking lot or the company who made the wheels, whoever has the money. As long as the lawyers get paid, justice has been done.

The "Short" Scam

Burn private business, it's a peaceful protest. Storm the Capital, it's an insurrection. Scam a million individual investors of a few billion dollars, it's market forces. Individual investors use social media to turn the tables on a multi-billion-dollar hedge-fund short scam, trading is suspended, and their social media accounts are shut down.

Multi-billion-dollar hedge-fund corporations "donate" to elected officials in exchange for laws that allow them to suck more billions out of the system, part of which finances more donations. One of those laws lets them borrow against a company's stock, stock that is owned by individual investors who don't pay government officials for preferential treatment.

The "contract" lets them borrow the value of the stock, with a promise to repay it at a later date, at its later value. It the stock goes up, they lose money, but if they borrow on enough of a company's stock, it forces the stock down. If they short all of it, or even more than 100 percent, it will force the stock to zero, bankrupt the company and the hedge fund repays nothing. The individual investors lose everything.

It's simple. But you won't hear that story from any of the corporate media talking heads who act like they support the little guy. The hedge funds have been pulling this scam for years. Every one of those talking heads knew it. But their employers share in the take which trickles down to their salaries.

It's just one of the thousands of ways our corrupt ruling class steal from the only source of real wealth in this country, people who work. Our system as articulated in the Constitution, allowed working Americans to create more wealth than any nation in history. It was just too much temptation for those in power.

In the twelve months between July 2020 and July 2021 the Federal Reserve created 8.2 trillion new U.S. dollars. Over the same period the total value of the stock market increased by 8.2 trillion dollars. Over the same period the government spent 8.2 trillion dollars. They bought 40 billion dollars-worth of mortgages every month, subsidized cities who had defunded their police departments and paid employees not to return to work at small businesses, 38 percent of which had permanently closed over the same period.

It was the largest and fastest transfer of wealth in history and it inflated a bubble that, when it bursts, will cascade across the globe destroying every economy, government and currency on the planet, and it is not an accident.

Free Press

The Free Press has been replaced by a New York based corporate media conglomerate that is piped into over ninety percent of American homes. There are no market forces. Basic programing packages force every subscriber to support sanctioned information outlets they don't want or agree with. Every subscriber is forced to pay media outlets whose anchors and contributors swap places with government officials so often that it's hard to tell one institution from the other.

Most of them are blatant and unapologetic like NBC, CBS, ABC and CNN. Fox News and Fox Business are part of the same billionaire-run media, but their target audience is farther from the fold and subjected to more nuanced persuasion. They'll spend three days covering breaking news they could have explained in four minutes because, it's hard to produce programing for twenty-four hours a day when you can't talk about six hundred political prisoners who are in solitary confinement for trying to stop the steal the "free press" failed to report.

They can't talk about the CIA, Federal Reserve or the covertly unified one-party political system. They report on Climate Change with talking points because an actual investigation of facts would offend their corporate advertisers. So, they hope for a new terror attack or a natural disaster and report on what flavor ice cream Biden ate today.

They tell us what to believe, and while that doesn't usually work on an individual basis, it is very effective at giving the impression that most people do believe it. And that's how you get away with assassinating the President, stealing trillions of dollars and rigging a presidential election. That's how you lose a country.

When a corrupt justice department covered for President Kennedy's murderers, a free press would have investigated. Our press was complicit. When Hillary Clinton concocted and paid for a fake Trump-Russia connection, our press was complicit. When the FBI conducted an illegal sting operation on an incoming President and his staff, our press was complicit.

When poll watchers and reporters were sent home late on election night so that hundreds of thousands of forged ballots could be brought in and counted for the ruling class's candidate, the sanctioned press was complicit.

When Covid-19 was used to bankrupt several million small businesses while no large corporation closed, the media said nothing. When schools were closed causing untold damage to millions of children as a tool for the Teacher's Union after we knew that kids didn't spread and weren't susceptible to the virus, the media said nothing. When it was learned that the virus was created in a Chinese lab, the media paraded a string of witnesses for almost a year who testified that it was not possible.

The revolving door between Congress, Cabinet officials, Directors of alphabet agencies and news outlets is dwarfed by the millions and billions of dollars that flow through corporations, foundations foreign governments and sanctioned media to influence trillions of taxpayer dollars paid by small business and working people who then must pay for the news outlets to tell us the United States should be ashamed of our wealth, our freedom and especially the energy we burn.

Director of National Intelligence James Clapper testified under oath to Congress that the agency was not spying on Americans. Edward Snowden released evidence that the NSA was spying on Americans. A warrant was issued for Snowden's arrest. Clapper got a job on CNN. The Taliban has a million followers on twitter, but a President of the United States that seventy-five million Americans voted for, more votes than any man in history, is banned. It's time to quit pretending that we live in a free country.

Capitalism

Everything should be divided equally. Sounds fair. If you see people who have much more than you, it seems like it would be to your advantage. The problem is, the only way to accomplish it is by force. A few people must have enough power to control what everyone else is allowed to have. It will always concentrate most of the wealth and power in the hands of the few. Every time someone in power says, "those people have too much, we should take some of it for the disadvantaged." What they mean is "those people have, and I want the power to take it."

A free enterprise system is one in which no one can use force to gain economic power. All transactions are entered into voluntarily by all parties. It is the most successful system ever tried. It has lifted more people out of poverty than all the welfare schemes in history. It spreads wealth across all segments of society. When unencumbered by excessive taxes and regulations, more producers make more stuff and compete for custom. This competition weeds out less dependable producers, eliminates inferior products and provides more choices for consumers. It is the only economic system that has ever led to a continuously expanding and sustainable prosperity.

As government grows, more product is controlled by government, made by fewer producers. The people share a smaller pool of goods, have fewer choices and undependable producers have little if any incentive to improve. Inferior products persist without competition.

An idea as simple as empowering the individual changed the world because it is human nature to want to make something. Whether you do it with a hammer, brush or lawn mower, a job done well feels good. It feels better when others like what we made, and better yet when they want it enough to give you something of value for it. Capitalism is in our DNA. It works because everyone involved feels good. The guy who grows hops and barley, is proud when his work comes to fruition. The woman who pays him for his hops and barley feels pride in the beer she sells to a man who is glad to trade a share of what he earned trimming another man's grass for a glass of cold beer at the end of the day. It created more opportunity for more people at every step which compounds like interest and grew into the wealthiest economy the world has ever seen.

When someone is successful and accumulates wealth, it attracts people who want some of it. The best way to get it, is to make something of value that the successful guy needs or wants, which makes more successful people who each create opportunity for more people to become successful. The essence of a free society is that success comes to those who please others. It doesn't make everyone rich, but it gives everyone an opportunity to become rich, by pleasing more people, by providing a product or service that more people want at a price they want to pay. This system creates more wealth than anything that's ever been tried. Taxing this system moderately can help far more of those unable to take advantage of opportunity than politicians will ever help by taxing millionaires and billionaires.

Wealth is a great temptation to those who would take some of it by force.

In a society that has no rich people, no one can get rich. If we want it to be possible for us or our children or grandchildren to be successful, we must support the existence of other successful people, as long as their success was earned by pleasing people and not stolen through the use of force. The most important decision any government makes is whether to let productive citizens keep most of what they earn or take it under the theory that the general good will be better served if government bureaucrats spend it. It is the nature of politicians to offer higher wages, better jobs, health care, all kinds of things, if they are just allowed to confiscate more of what people earn. The history of the world is rife with what happens when they do.

An economic and political system that allows private individuals to earn and keep their own property, organically provides opportunity to everyone indiscriminately and has built in regulation enforced by individual choice. The grocer who sells rotten food is put out of business by his customers. In a regulated system, we all get stuck paying the same phone company, no choice. Free enterprise capitalism has natural checks and balances that have no prejudices. It creates opportunity organically which is available without prejudice to anyone willing and able to take advantage of it. It is not equal opportunity because people are not equal. Ugly girls don't become cheerleaders and fat guys don't get the leading role in an action film, but fat guys and ugly girls will succeed at something else as long as the government doesn't try to fix the cheer leading and movie problem.

Advocates of Socialism complain that many miss out on the opportunities inherent in free enterprise, and that's true. They do not recognize opportunity when it is all around them because more often than not it comes disguised as hard work. Even so, it sounds reasonable to tax those who do succeed in order to help those who miss out. Our own government is glaring proof that it doesn't work because of the unavoidable fundamental fact that money sticks to the fingers of the ruling class as it makes its way from the taxpayer to its intended use.

The United States has always been a blend of Capitalism (free markets) and Socialism (schools, roads, welfare, social security, etc.) As founded, the United States was almost entirely a Capitalist system, burdened by a minimum of social obligations. Today it is a Socialist system where a shrinking free enterprise is asked to support it.

I have spent most of the last 40 years building a small manufacturing business. The year I sold it, 2018, it produced 3.8 million dollars-worth of product that people choose to pay for. In each of those 40 years, the government demanded a larger share of what we produced and enforced more rules about how we could produce it. Somewhere along the way I realized that my government believed that small business was its enemy. I watched hundreds of small to medium sized businesses move their manufacturing to Mexico, South America, China and India to escape the government's wrath.

The government doesn't create any wealth. The only way wealth has ever been created is by someone doing work of some kind to make something of value. 30 percent of my factory's revenue each year went to employee wages and expenses. My employees took home about half of it, the government in its various forms took the rest. You might think that a system that taxes work would encourage work, but every time I hired someone, I paid a penalty. Every time I even gave someone a raise, my company was penalized by the government.

In the words of Thomas Jefferson "*Rightful liberty is unobstructed action according to our will within the limits drawn around us by the equal rights of others*" The result of creating a political system based on this sentiment was little short of a miracle. The Constitution was written in a few pages of plain language that any literate person can understand. It states clearly and simply what the government can do and more importantly, what it cannot do. There is no need for constitutional scholars. It is a simple tool that does an exceptionally good job of doing the simple, singular job it was designed to do, defending the individual liberty of United States citizens. But like any tool, it is only as good as the people who use it.

Today it is prejudiced by campaign contributions and lobbyists. Under this system large multinational corporations pay little if any federal taxes while, I know first-hand, small business is so heavily burdened by taxes and regulations as to make it virtually impossible to succeed. It is easy to shake our heads at the waste and stupidity of government, but it is not stupidity, it is organized theft on a scale never before seen in human history.

When the big bank monopoly in New York crashed our banking system in 2008, there were over a hundred federal regulatory entities with oversight authority over those banks. Millions of overpaid bureaucrats not only failed to prevent the crash, but they also didn't even see it coming. President Bush and 535 members of Congress, many of whom sat on committees overseeing or investigating the banks were equally clueless.

These people are not equipped to control our economy, but they're doing it anyway. They have borrowed 30 trillion dollars, $200,000 per taxpayer, and their only plan is to borrow more. They are taking over more of the economy every year. Before the 2008 crash, the federal government owned about half of all residential mortgages. By 2019 it was well over 90 percent. They have taken over the student loan industry and are taking over the health care industry. Just a few of the thousands of ways they are displacing free enterprise.

The federal government will default on its debt. There is a maximum effective tax rate after which more taxes decrease economic activity slowing tax revenue. The honest, mathematical truth is, they have already borrowed more than any tax rate could repay. A world-wide economic collapse is inevitable. It will be the most traumatic event to face the world since the Great Depression.

The ironic thing is, they didn't really borrow 30 trillion dollars. How could they have? Where would the wealthiest nation on Earth go to borrow that much money? The answer is no one on this planet bought 30 trillion dollars-worth of treasury securities. Remember, they would have had to sell $200,000 worth of treasury bonds to every wage earner in the United States, it's just not realistic.

The scam looks like this. Every time Congress raises the debt ceiling, the Federal Reserve adds that amount to its balance sheet. Since there aren't enough lenders in the world to buy that many treasury bonds the Fed liquidates the money they just added and distributes it to a handful of big banks with strings that cause them to invest it in U.S. treasuries. We the Taxpayers are paying interest on money that wasn't really borrowed. It's a win for the banks who collect interest, Congress who collects contributions to influence how they will spend it, and whoever makes $500 hammers, $2,000 toilets and bridges to nowhere. The losers are anyone with a job and the next several generations of Americans.

Politicians promise to take out undeserving millionaires and billionaires to pay for all kinds of stuff for the American people. The stuff never turns out as good as they promised, it always cost more than they said it would and the working masses always end up paying for it. Working people always have and always will pay for the schemes of greedy politicians. That's why taxes are deducted from pay checks, because that's where the real wealth is produced.

Illegal Immigration

This is another example of who really runs this country. The third world population on this planet grows by 100 million people every 18 months. In 2021, several million of them from 150 countries were flown to Mexico where over two million of them entered the U.S. illegally. They were then flown by the U.S. military to states that voted for Trump in the 2020 election. They're being used to dilute the value of U.S. citizenship. To take the country away from Americans so it could be sublimed into socialist world government, but that's not why they come here. They come here because they can make more money in an hour in the United States than in a week where they come from.

The large manufacturing corporations moved their factories to other countries years ago, but corporate food producers didn't have that luxury. A large segment of food production in the United States is controlled by a handful of global corporations. The Chinese Communist Party Inc. owns close to thirty percent of the farmland. The country's largest food producers employ the largest number of illegal aliens, contribute the most money to members of Congress who sit on two committees, the Agriculture Committee and the Subcommittee on Immigration and Citizenship. They are also the end recipients multi-trillion-dollar government food subsidies.

A large majority of U.S. citizens, including immigrants, support enforcement of U.S. immigration law. If those laws were enforced, employers who hired illegals would be arrested, fined and/or jailed and most illegals would head out for places they could earn a meal. That's assuming of course that we didn't issue them all free health care, day care, an EBT card and a driver's license. U.S. citizens don't run this country though, large, global largely Chinese owned corporations run this country. So, while illegal immigrants who come here and commit additional crimes are given due process, along with their free health care, day care, EBT card and driver's license, U.S. citizens are held in solitary confinement for trespassing on public property.

Accurate numbers are hard to come by because our rulers don't want us to know how many people they have allowed in illegally. We do know that the U.S. population has increased by 100 million people in 30 years. We know that English is no longer the primary language in most southern and western U.S. cities. We know that the government information machine is telling us that requiring voters to prove they are U.S. citizens is racist.

How many is too many? If the goal was to assimilate diverse people into the traditions of individual liberty and equal opportunity that made America a place people want to come to in the first place, then the first person who violated our laws to enter the country was too many.

The Biden administration suspended U.S. law on the pretense that conditions in Guatemala, El Salvador and Honduras are so violent and economically disadvantaged that is justified on humanitarian grounds. The fact is several U.S. cities have a higher murder rate than any of those countries and the police in these cities readily admit that drug dealing gangs control the streets.

During the four years between 2016 and 2020 human trafficking and slave trade between South America and Mexico decreased by 50 percent and the two competing drug cartels for whom the United States is a primary market saw their business reduced by over fifty percent. It all resumed with a vengeance in 2021 in an effort to increase the poor, brown segment of the population before the next election.

The ruling class in America have become rich and powerful borrowing on the future production of the American people to the tune of $250,000 per working person as of 2021. Our ruler's problem is simple, they need more working people. More importantly, they need to dilute the number of people who value principles of freedom and liberty because free people wouldn't continue to work harder for less every year to support the luxurious lifestyle of their leaders.

The best way to export our higher standard of living to the world was to spread free enterprise and individual liberty, but the last thing multi-national corporations working to expand their global monopolies want is a free and strong United States. They certainly can't allow freedom to spread into the rest of the world where their coal powered, four dollar a day factories pour chemical waste into the world's rivers and oceans.

Instead of spreading freedom to the rest of the world, the goal of the people who propped Joe Biden up in the White House is to kill it in the United States. The 30 million or so mostly Mexican, South American and Middle Eastern illegals in this country are a dead-man's switch that when tripped will instantly nullify the votes of working-class Americans independent farmers and small businessmen. They intend to flip that switch before November 2024 which is why they ceased all enforcement on the border and invited a new surge of immigrants.

One of the few enumerated powers and responsibilities our Constitution gives the federal government is that of protecting our country from foreign adversaries. Defending U.S. borders is the legal role of the military. Instead, our southern border has been erased while the military builds walls, roads, schools, hospitals and serves as policemen in foreign lands to support a global industrial complex.

When the powers that control our elections proffered George W. Bush and Al Gore as choices in the 2000 election, I assumed Bush was the least dangerous. When he used the 9/11 attacks to start two or three unrelated wars and expand federal power with the deceptively named Patriot Act and the creation of yet another unconstitutional department, the Department of Homeland (Internal) Security, we should have all realized that we have had no choice for some time. The 2016 election was an anomaly, and it will never be allowed again.

If Congress ever passes an immigration bill, it will be written by our enemies, cost ten trillion dollars and be printed on six thousand pages that no one will ever read. An immigration bill written in the interests of U.S. citizens could consist of two paragraphs and would not only cost nothing, it would save tax dollars.

D.H.S. would be liquidated as part of the bankruptcy of an obviously insolvent federal government. Immigration, Border Patrol, T.S.A, the Secret Service would be folded into the Coast Guard. The rest of the military would vacate at least a hundred of the 116 countries where they are currently deployed and concentrate on protecting the sovereignty of U.S. citizens.

Once the border has been secured and immigration law enforced, a statute of limitation could be discussed for those who entered illegally up to some point in the past, subject only to those who have not been involved in additional criminal activity. All others will be returned to their country of origin to apply for legal immigration.

Of course, that kind of law would require an honest election and I seriously doubt we'll ever see another one of those.

National Debt

"The last official act of any government is to loot the treasury."

George Washington

Where does the wealthiest nation on Earth go to borrow 30 trillion dollars? There is no such place. The Federal Reserve conjured it out of smoke and mirrors. Most of our government's debt is owed to the privately owned Federal Reserve. The Federal Reserve controls the interest rate and so dictates how much we all pay in interest on the debt. A one percent rate increase raises the interest payment by nearly half a trillion dollars, and since the money to pay the interest must also be borrowed from the Federal Reserve, the act of making the payment, increases the debt. It sounds like a scam because it is a scam.

In September of 2020, the Congressional Budget Office warned that the federal debt would reach 29 trillion by 2028. The debt passed 29 trillion in 2021. The world's economy depends on the predictability of the value of money. If the CBO was off by eight years, in twelve months, something is very wrong. Money is a substitute for trust among strangers. Without that trust, the 330 million people who make up the U.S. economy will be reduced to bartering with neighbors, an economic regression of about a thousand years.

The U.S. government is insolvent. It's obvious to anyone who has ever done a budget. There is no way U.S. taxpayers could repay the thirty trillion dollars Congress has borrowed in our name, but it's much worse than that. Congress has actually obligated U.S. taxpayers with over 300 trillion dollars in debt and other unfunded obligations.

Most Americans are aware that most politicians and bureaucrats can't be trusted. A quick count of the number of people who have become millionaires and billionaires after being elected or appointed to public office will give an accurate estimate of just how many are involved. Using that method, we have determined that eighty percent of federal officeholders are crooks. The scale of their corruption can be accurately estimated by the discrepancy between the amount of revenue they have been able to legitimately collect, and the amount of money that has disappeared into the bureaucratic quagmire without anything to show for it, the national debt.

This nations greatness is its wealth, more accurately it is the wealth of its free people. Everything the United States has accomplished in over 200 years from defeating the British, Imperial Japan and the Third Reich to putting men on the Moon was paid for by American workers. As the American people's wealth is stolen, the nation becomes weaker. This country's wealth and strength are evaporating before our eyes.

The debt that those in power are incurring, is not their debt. It is not based on their intention of ever repaying it. It's based on the promise that future American workers will repay it.

The debt doesn't represent something of value received by the American people. In fact, there is a direct anti-correlation between excess government spending and the economic and cultural security of the average U. S. Citizen, and there is a direct correlation between the 30 trillion dollars that we are obligated to repay, and the wealth accumulated by those in power.

The nature of embezzlement is that it is disguised as something innocent. Otherwise, they would just pass a law ceding every American's property immediately to the few hundred powerful people who make up our ruling class. As long as they keep the American people divided, they can convince half of us that their corrupt programs are lifesaving, and that reform would kill people.

In December of 2019, while the Senate held hearings on Justice Department abuse that reaches the highest-ranking law enforcement officials in government, and the House voted on Articles of Impeachment, Democrats and Republicans at each other's throats, quietly and innocuously slipped another few trillion dollars out of the pockets of American workers present and future. That was just the beginning. Over the next two years they spent over $75,000 per taxpayer, and make no mistake, the act of spending is the tax. What they claim the tax rate is, is just another lie. We were obligated to cover every dollar the instant they spent it.

There was no debate. Republicans got everything they wanted, Democrats got everything they wanted, and we got another ten trillion dollars in debt. In just 16 months, during a period that saw the greatest division between the two parties since the 1850's, they managed to find enough common ground to spend enough to erase the incomes of every middle-class taxpayer in America. Not a word about what it cost or who will pay for it. It was not an isolated incident, it's what they do.

Members of Congress inexplicably become multi-millionaires while "serving" because they are embezzling public funds on a scale that has bankrupted the U.S. government and destroyed our country. Every member of Congress who voted to borrow another dime on our backs while we are not at war is guilty of treason. The appearance of solvency is an illusion dependent on monetary tricks performed by the Federal Reserve. The illusion of justice is impossible to maintain when our property, the proceeds of our labor, belongs by default to our rulers.

Taxes

Anyone who says they will tax the rich is a liar. The rich have never paid taxes and they never will. That is true throughout history and in every country on the planet. The rich move or move their money to other jurisdictions if they can't bribe those in power to exempt them.

Honestly, that's how it must be. The rich have too much influence to be forced to pay the costs of government. The only way the rich have ever paid their share is when it is the same share everyone else pays.

Thomas Paine wrote, on the necessity of taxes, that "he finds it necessary to surrender up a part of his property to furnish means for the protection of the rest." That is a solid reason to pay taxes. The purpose of democracy is to ensure that the rest of us are also entitled to the same deal.

Article 1, Section 2 "Direct Taxes shall be apportioned among the several States which may be included within this Union, according to their respective numbers"

Article 1, Section 8 "All Duties, Imposts and Excises shall be uniform throughout the United States"

Article 1, Section 9 "No Capitation, or other direct Tax shall be laid unless in proportion to the Census or Enumeration herein before directed to be taken"

If the Constitution was law, our government would collect and spend our money in the most efficient manner possible, the burden would be shared evenly with our fellow citizens, and it would be done in a manner that respects our life, liberty and property. If the Constitution was the law, everyone would be taxed by the same rules as everyone else.

Unfortunately, the law is over 80,000 pages of Statutes, Regulations and Caselaw that offer ample opportunity for anyone with enough money to exempt themselves from the rules that apply to the rest of us. We no longer voluntarily surrender a portion of our property to protect the rest, we submit to force.

We have strayed so far from our founding that it is illegal in the United States to pay for and own a home outright, or even a piece of land. The Arkansas Constitution states: "Property taxes constitute a lien on property and bind that property from the first Monday in January of the assessment year until taxes are paid in the collection year".

That means that on the first business date in January of this year, the state put a lean on everyone's property that stays in effect until we pay this year's taxes, next year, by which time the state will have already placed another lien on all our property.

Owning a piece of property gives you the opportunity to improve it, to turn your labor into value, to profit without anyone or anything between you and your success. But in Arkansas, and every other State, no one can own a home or the ground it sets on.

Each year Arkansas' 75 counties spend several hundred million dollars assessing, re-assessing and collecting property taxes. The state could net the same revenue by collecting less than half the taxes using the existing sales tax system while putting the decision of when and how much to pay in the hands of taxpayers instead of tax collectors.

The immorality of the property tax will become apparent when the nation's debt reaches its inevitable conclusion. People who have worked a lifetime will learn that everything they paid into Social Security was stolen, then they will be evicted from the home they spent thirty or more years paying for by the State who, it turns out, really owns it.

Social Security:

The federal government can collect income taxes because of the 16th Amendment, we'll ignore for now, the fact that that amendment was not passed legally. It collects Social Security taxes on the authority of an act of Congress. When the Act was passed, they promised that 1% of our earnings was all it would ever cost. Even in 1937 it was really 2% because our employers had to match it. Today it cost every worker 15.3%.

It is easy to assume that Social Security was started with good intentions, only to become corrupted by bureaucracy as the years passed. It could have been, was even close to being, what it promised. A "comprehensive package of protection" against the "hazards and vicissitudes of life." Except that from the beginning, it was designed as a scheme to raise taxes at a time, in the midst of the depression, when raising taxes would have been politically difficult. There were no beneficiaries in the beginning, because no one had paid into the system yet. All of the money was 'invested' in Federal Savings Bonds, which was in effect federal debt that allowed Congress to spend money. As people began to draw out of the system, withholdings were increased to cover the payments, but the "trust fund" was continuously replaced with I.O.U.'s as contributions evaporated to serve the true purpose of the program.

Today Social Security confiscates enough of an average workers lifetime pay to finance a million-dollar retirement in exchange for a promise of $1,500 dollars or so per month at retirement. We get that promise instead of a lockbox with our money in it, because the money is wasted or stolen as fast as it is withheld from our pay. On the day we retire, there is exactly nothing left. Older people who depend on the money aren't inclined to complain, and working people aren't in a position to complain, it's the perfect Ponzi Scheme that targets the middle class. Income from investments, dividends, interest and capital gains, in other words income more common to the wealthy, are exempt. The fact that your employer pays half of your contribution might make it look like a good deal, but it doesn't change the math. The cost of the system, plus interest compounded over a lifetime of work, equals far more than any of us will ever collect from the Social Security System.

Saving for retirement is an important thing. Trusting our savings to the federal government was a terrible idea. If the money that an average American worker paid into the Social Security system would have been invested in rolling certificates of deposit accounts at an average interest rate of 3.8 percent, a conservative number considering historical rates, his retirement account would be worth close to a million dollars today. Enough to retire at age 59 and collect $4,600 per month for 30 years.

Since he sent that money to the government instead of a bank, it's all gone. It has been replaced with a promise from a government that is mathematically bankrupt to pay about $1,400 per month beginning at age 65 or so. A promise that is dependent on taxing more younger workers every year. That is the definition of a Ponzi scheme which is also by definition, a fraud.

The idea of privatizing Social Security has been stigmatized by the people who have stolen the difference between what our contributions are worth, and what the system has to show for it, which is effectively nothing since they now need to steal from new marks to hide the loss.

The problem with Social Security is the same as the problem with the national debt. It was stolen, and theft on that scale makes the thieves more powerful than the people. Our Republic has been usurped and the usurpers are far too wealthy to let a little thing like freedom or the Constitution get in their way. We need to get future Social Security dollars out of the hands of government. Our nation's founders had the foresight, wisdom and Common Sense to tell us how to do it, the tenth Amendment.

If any one of our 50 Governors had the guts to intercept Social Security withholding dollars and hire a reputable financial services company with fiduciary responsibility to manage a retirement fund within the State, it would have the effect of pulling the last straw out from under the fraud our government is perpetrating on working Americans.

All of the time and money spent defending First and Second Amendment rights will be wasted if we continue to allow the Tenth Amendment to be violated with impunity. It is the most important amendment in the Bill of Rights. Without the Tenth Amendment, the others are meaningless, and yet each year trillions are made off of its violation. That's why the government is closing in on 30 trillion in debt. It's why the government is bankrupt, and it's why freedom is dying in America.

The current tax code consists of over four million words, more than six times longer than the Bible. It requires 25 volumes to contain it and takes up nine feet of shelf space. All based entirely on the 16th Amendment, which authorizes Congress "to lay and collect taxes on incomes, from whatever source derived."

A group of billionaire bankers and crooked politicians told the American people that the 16th Amendment would only apply to the top one percent. It was time for the rich to pay their fair share.

In 1913 the meaning of the word "income" was clearly understood, and it did not apply to wages and salaries. Proponents of the 16th Amendment cited the 1910 edition of Black's Dictionary of Law which defined income tax as "A tax on the yearly profits arising from property, professions, trades, and offices."

They used the Judicial and Statutory Definition of Words and Phrases, published in 1904 by West Publishing Co. which defined "income tax" as a "tax which relates to the product or income from property or from business pursuits.

As written, advertised and ratified, the 16th amendment applied only to profit from investments, dividends, interest and capital gains. there is absolutely no constitutional authority for our wages or salaries to be taxed, and they still weren't able to get the thing legally ratified.

In "The Law That Never Was," Bill Benson made a convincing case that the 16th amendment was not legally ratified, and that Secretary of State Philander Knox was not merely in error but committed fraud when he declared it ratified in February 1913.

Congress passed the 16th Amendment in 1909 and sent it to the states for ratification by the legislatures. There were 48 states at the time, and three-fourths, or 36, of them were required for it to be ratified. The process took most of four years. Knox counted 38 states as having approved the Amendment.

The Kentucky legislature acted on the amendment without having received it from the governor. The version of the amendment that the Kentucky legislature acted upon omitted the words "on income" from the text, so they weren't even voting on an income tax. Later, when the text was corrected, the Kentucky senate rejected the amendment. Philander Knox counted Kentucky as approving it anyway.

The Oklahoma legislature changed the wording of the amendment so that its meaning was virtually the opposite of what Congress had passed. This was the version they sent back to Knox who counted Oklahoma as approving it, despite a memo from his chief legal counsel, Reuben Clark, that states were not allowed to change it in any way.

The state constitution of Tennessee prohibited the state legislature from acting on any proposed amendment to the U.S. Constitution sent by Congress until after the next election of state legislators. They acted upon it illegally before they were authorized to do so. They also violated their own state constitution by failing to read the resolution on three different days as prescribed by Article II, Section 18. These state constitutional violations make their approval of the amendment invalid.

107

Texas and Louisiana violated provisions in their state constitutions prohibiting the legislatures from empowering the federal government with any additional taxing authority.

Twelve other states, besides Tennessee, violated provisions in their constitutions requiring that a bill be read on three different days before voting on it. Mississippi, Ohio, Arkansas, Minnesota, New Mexico, West Virginia, Indiana, Nevada, North Carolina, North Dakota, Colorado, and Illinois.

When Secretary Knox transmitted the proposed amendment to the states, official certified and sealed copies were sent. Likewise, when state results were returned to Knox, it was required that the documents, including the resolution that was actually approved, be properly certified, signed, and sealed by the appropriate officials. A number of states returned uncertified, unsigned, and/or unsealed copies, and did not rectify their negligence even after being reminded and warned by Knox. The most egregious offenders were Ohio, California, Arkansas, Mississippi, and Minnesota which did not send any copy at all.

There were other anomalies including state constitutions that limited the taxing authority of their legislatures, which could not give to the federal government authority they did not have, that reinforced the conclusion that the amendment was not legally ratified.

The federal budget in 1910 was one billion dollars. They financed it with taxes on imports which gave American manufacturers an advantage which created jobs and grew our economy which created more demand for imports and increased federal revenues at a pace consistent with the growth of the country.

The ratification of the 16th Amendment was certified under dubious circumstances, the definition of income was changed, the wages of workers were attached, and the government rid itself of restraints. The only restraint they were left with was how fast they could confiscate private property without causing a revolt.

Health Care

When the Affordable Care Act was passed, my wife and I were able to grandfather in our existing Arkansas Blue Cross insurance. The premiums went up each January by whatever amount the Arkansas Insurance Department approved, 9.9 percent for 2020. I retired in 2018, leaving me with assets, but considerably less income. So, I checked out Healthcare.gov where I found another Arkansas Blue Cross policy that was more than twice the cost of our current policy, but with a tax subsidy that would make our premiums about half of what we were paying. Two days later I received a cancellation notice for our old policy. I hadn't signed up for the new policy, why was Blue Cross so eager to cancel our old policy? How did they know I looked at a new policy?

Blue Cross wanted us out of our old policy even though its cost had nearly doubled since we bought it on the free market, because they will collect twice as much under the new policy. Blue Cross Blue Shield is the largest lobbyist in the health care industry. Along with other large insurance corporations, they spent millions on contributions to lobbyist and members of Congress during the months that the Affordable Care Act was written. The return on that investment has been far greater than any legitimate investment they could have made.

This illustrates perfectly the flaw in our system, and it explains why our government is 30 trillion dollars in debt even though many elections have been won on promises to cut spending.

Every dollar Congress spends is controlled by thousands of multi-million-dollar influence brokers who sell their product on behalf of their clients who include practically every large business, union and "charitable" organization and foundation in the country as well as a host of foreign governments, which explains why our government sends our money to almost two hundred foreign countries. Every time Congress spends billions of dollars, it benefits big business, unions, charitable organizations, foundations and foreign governments. Every time Congress spends billions of dollars, members of Congress grow wealthier. Every time Congress spends billions of dollars, we lose more of our property.

If you define success as a government program that provides a benefit to U.S. citizens greater than it's cost to U.S. citizens, the system itself precludes a successful outcome for any government program that spends any money at all.

In order to bypass the lobbyists, successful health care legislation would need to enact guidelines without spending federal dollars, but then Members of Congress would have to live on their salaries alone and lobbyist would have to find productive employment. Government spending would go down. Taxes would go down and health insurance companies and health care providers would compete to provide the best care at the lowest cost.

We could start by doing the same thing to education. Part of our county's health care problem is the skyrocketing cost and declining value of higher education which is the result of the same systemic flaw that has crippled our health care system. The current federal student loan program inflates the cost of education and encourages students to go into debt for an education that won't earn enough money to repay the loans so that professors, administrators and especially politicians can take millions out of the system.

If you took federal dollars out of the education system, schools would be forced to compete for students by providing a better product at a lower cost. Students with good grades would be able to borrow money to study medicine because the future return would make it a good risk for a bank or other investor. The system would regulate itself without taxpayer dollars or bureaucratic interference and it would force thousands more influence peddlers and bureaucrats to get real jobs.

Insurance companies, while free to offer any kind of policy they please would compete to offer policies that cover only more serious and less likely medical events for people who pay cash for minor medical needs. Employers would be free to offer any benefits they believe would attract better employees, but these benefits would be treated like any other income for tax purposes. An employer who wants to pay a higher wage instead of offering benefits should not be penalized.

As for pre-existing illnesses, a quick once over of the U.S. Constitution should be enough to convince anyone with Common Sense that the federal government has no jurisdiction in the matter. State lawmakers do have jurisdiction, and many of them will come up with great, cost-effective programs to deal with it. Those that don't will probably join their colleagues looking for more appropriate employment after the next election.

Modern Medicine has increased lifespans across the world and particularly in the United States by decades. The question is, should medicine be left to private industry, or managed by government? If it is left to private industry, the profit motive will fuel continued advances. In the long run there is no practical limit on how long a person could live if they are willing to pay for it.

That is the rub then. As a society, are we willing to give up those advances in order to keep rich people from buying longer lives than the rest of us? A short sighted and selfish society certainly would. It's not fair for everyone, but without a profit motive, those advances won't come. With a profit motive, only the rich will benefit at first, but then the advances will be available to a growing segment of society forever. It will in the long run benefit almost everyone. On the other hand, if we allow government to keep things fair from the start, the advances will stop, and lifespans will be stagnant for everyone equally.

As for the drawbacks of longer life spans, nature is a wonderfully self-regulating system. The advances that would drastically increase human lifespans are only possible if they are initially available to a very few. As soon as you mandate that they be made available to everyone, they don't happen in the first place. If nature is allowed progress unencumbered by bureaucrats who know more than God, the space, impact on the environment and other problems associated with longer lifespans will be resolved with parallel advances in managed reproduction, living space advances and extraterrestrial exploration.

Free enterprise did create the best health care system in the world and most of us will live longer for it. Now the ruling class controls our health care system, and two things are certain. One, the ruling class will live longer. Two, the rest of us will have equity.

Lies

This book is based on the premise that the worlds government/corporate hierarchy is involved in an organized effort to establish a single socialist world government designed to harvest the labor of the masses to support an elite and unimaginably wealthy ruling class. In order to accomplish this, the ruling class has perpetrated a vast scam on free people everywhere. The scope of the deceit is hard to believe. To help put it into perspective, I have compiled a partial list of lies we have been told by our government.

Beginning with the first lie all but five or six of them tell as they take office.

I do solemnly swear that I will support and defend the Constitution of the United States against all enemies, foreign and domestic; that I will bear true faith and allegiance to the same; that I take this obligation freely, without any mental reservation or purpose of evasion; and that I will well and faithfully discharge the duties of the office on which I am about to enter: So help me God.

The rich will pay their fair share. (they've told that one every two years for over 120 years)

The government does not collect the telephone records of millions of Americans, "not wittingly"

We just need two weeks to bend the curve.

If we don't give up our cars, meat and airplanes, cities will sink into the sea.

Covid doesn't spread at BLM riots.

Hunter's computer was planted by Russian agents.

If you are fully vaccinated, you no longer need to wear a mask. Masks prevent the spread of Covid. Shutdowns will slow the spread.

Trump rallies are super spreader events.

Social Security will only cost one percent of your wages, that's all you will ever pay. The money will be kept in a lock box for your use in your old age.

The Kennedy brothers were each killed by disturbed lone gunmen.

A million Trump supporters protesting a stolen election was an insurrection. (Of course, it was. Thousands of people have rigged elections, it still happens every year, and every one of them calls the poor schlubs who thought the election should have been honest, insurrectionists.)

America is a racist country.

If you like your doctor, you can keep your doctor.

The greatest threat to our country are white supremacists. (They've been using that one for thousands of years. When your inept and dishonest leadership can't solve the problem, blame the witches. The church tortured and burned a half million of them for causing the weather, plagues, crop failures, hang nails.)

The greatest threat facing our way of life is communism. (Our leaders, like the church before them, tried to defeat an idea that would have failed on its own by burning people, whose huts just happened to be on land that could be put to better use by Standard Oil or Exxon-Mobile.)

Some of the most atrocious lies were told so we would submit to the government sacrificing tens of thousands of our children in one war or another, usually fought for corporate profits. As of 2016the U.S. military had more than 1,500,000 buildings at more than 10,000 locations on more than 60 million acres in 138 countries.

When the USS Maine exploded in Havana harbor in 1898, the captain, reported it as an accident resulting from an on-board fire.

President McKinley and the newspapers of the day claimed it was a Spanish attack because his creditors needed a war with Spain.

On May 7th, 1915, a German U-Boat sank the Lusitania. The ship was heavily subsidized by the British Government and designed to be converted into a military auxiliary cruiser. Germany declared that Lusitania was being used to transport military cargoes and took out ads in American newspapers warning civilians not to take passage on her. The ship was smuggling military munitions to England, Germany sunk her, and our government and the media lied to us so we would be OK with sacrificing 116,516 Americans in WWI.

Documents declassified in 1994 revealed that FDR followed an eight-step plan to provoke Japan into attacking Pearl Harbor because he wanted the U.S. in the war. The American people were told that the Japanese fleet-maintained radio silence, but Admiral Yamamoto's order to set sail for the attack was intercepted by the U.S. military on November 25th. A civilian radio operator on the steamship SS Lurline encountered the Japanese fleet and upon arrival in Honolulu provided a map to the Hawaiian Naval Intelligence office, three days before the attack. A newspaper headline in Honolulu warned of the attack a week before it occurred. I find it easy to believe that WWII was a necessary fight, at least the story we were told makes a good case, but if we have learned nothing else, it's that the story is not real.

On August 4th, 1964, an inexperienced sonar operator on the USS Maddox picked up the sounds of his own ship's screws and mistakenly interpreted them as incoming torpedoes. The Captain of the Maddox immediately reported the error up the chain of command, but the headlines reported that we had been attacked by North Vietnam. And that's how they convinced us that there was something in Vietnam worth 55,000 American lives.

In 2003 George W Bush claimed that Iraq had weapons of mass destruction. There was no evidence because Iraq did not have weapons of mass destruction, and Bush knew it. The U.N. had had inspectors in Iraq for weeks, they knew exactly what was and wasn't in Iraq. The evidence for WMD in Iraq was forged by Bush, Blair and the military industrial complex to convince the American people that there was something there worth killing or maiming 36,000 Americans.

In 2011, Barack Obama sent covert operatives into Libya to create civil unrest, then claimed it was a revolution to convince the American people that war with Libya was worth the lives of American soldiers.

A covert overthrow masquerading as a revolution justified U.S. troops in Syria.

When Saudi Arabians attacked the United States on 9/11, George W Bush escorted the bin Laden's back to Saudi Arabia before using the attacks as an excuse to invade Iraq.

The Bush administration invaded Afghanistan after a conglomerate of oil companies lobbied the Administration and Congress for a pipeline through that country. For twenty years the United States trained and armed Taliban forces disguised as Afghan soldiers. When the Biden Administration started withdrawing our troops, they took off their uniforms and shot at us with our own weapons.

Trump, and Jared Kushner had in place a plan to withdraw U.S. troops that hinged on peace agreements between many of Afghanistan's Middle East neighbors combined with pressure on China, whose opium business in Afghanistan is centuries old, and closing access to the world's largest market for China's opium, our southern border. It also involved keeping the Bagram Air Base, an important asset because of its proximity to China, Pakistan and Iran. Biden's overriding priority upon taking office was to dismantle everything Trump had put in place. So, when he withdrew U.S. forces he abandoned Bagram, leaving billions of dollars-worth of American weapons and supplies for the Taliban.

Fear and paranoia of Trump and the majority of Americans who did not elect him, caused Biden and the people around him to make many irrational decisions. Abandoning the Bagram Air Base will prove to be one of the costliest.

Ron Paul

Doctor Ron Paul served in the House of Representatives off and on from 1976 and 2013. He went to Washington to defend liberty and serve his constituents. He sold out to no one. He accomplished next to nothing because he didn't serve the ruling class. He left office saying that he hadn't thought freedom would be such a hard sell, but that wasn't the problem. Freedom didn't win because the ruling class didn't allow it.

In 2020, millions of Americans rallied across the country. They were clearly a threat to those in power. They were labeled enemies of the state, banned from social media and their votes were not counted.

In a 2011 speech in favor of a congressional resolution ordering the withdrawal of U.S. troops from Afghanistan Paul said "Should we leave Afghanistan? I think the answer is very clear, and it's not complicated. Of course, we should, as soon as we can. If we don't, we'll be there for another decade." He pointed out that the undeclared war had already cost a trillion dollars. Of course, he was right. Ten years, more than a thousand dead and another two trillion dollars later we did leave Afghanistan having accomplished nothing other than leaving the Taliban the third most well-equipped military in the world.

Dr. Paul continued. "Congress and especially as a House, we have reneged on our responsibilities. We have avoided our prerogatives of saying that we have the control. We have control of the purse. We have control of when we are supposed to go to war. Yet the wars continue. They never stop. And we are going to be completely brought down to our knees. We can't change Afghanistan. The people who are bragging about these changes, even if you could, you are not supposed to. You don't have the moral authority. You don't have the constitutional authority."

In January of 2021 Paul posted the following to his Facebook account. "Last week's massive social media purges — starting with President Trump's permanent ban from Twitter and other outlets — were shocking and chilling, particularly to those of us who value free expression and the free exchange of ideas." Ron Paul's Facebook account was blocked. The only opinions allowed are those that the ruling elites find acceptable. This is a no-opposition-allowed fascist state. That's why Congressman Paul made no headway in his decades long fight for liberty.

When Dr. Paul was running for president, in 2007, sanctioned media discovered that an accused "white supremacist had made a contribution to his campaign. When asked if he was going to send the money back? Paul said "No, I'm not. You just told me he's an unsavory character. Why should I return the money? He might use it for an unsavory purpose, while I'm going to use the money to advance the message of freedom."

Dr. Paul was one of many Americans to fight for liberty against the ruling class takeover. He inspired many more.

The No Big Bang Theory

An Alternative Theory of the Universe

The scientific establishment tends to conform to contemporary doctrine. Some of it is wrong. There was no Big Bang, the Universe is not expanding, and Reality exists whether we see it or not.

In 1919, after Einstein's prediction that gravity would bend light was confirmed experimentally, the New York Times printed the following: "Scientists who proclaim that space comes to an end somewhere are under some obligation to tell us what lies beyond it".

Einstein initially believed his universe to be finite and static. When it appeared to be expanding, scientists followed its past to an infinitely small point 14 billion years ago. Over the years institutional science has come up with one extraordinary fix after another to shoehorn every cosmological discovery for a hundred years into this finite three-dimensional Universe that apparently popped out of nothing 13.8 billion years ago.

It is generally accepted that the entire Universe existed as a point of zero size and infinite density or "Physically Paradoxical Singularity", a scientific way of saying that there's something wrong with this theory. It's paradoxical because they're missing something and the deeper we delve into the ramifications of General Relativity, the more obvious that becomes.

According to Einstein, when you approach a Black Hole or accelerate to near the speed of light, time passes more slowly for you than it does for the rest of the Universe. So slow that all of eternity will pass for the rest of the Universe before you reach the event horizon. In General Relativity space and time are so closely intertwined that you can't change one without affecting the other. When gravity slows the rate that time passes, space must slow as well. If three-dimensional space can slow, it must be moving.

In 1919 a mathematician named Theodor Kaluza attempted to incorporate an extra dimension into General Relativity. His five-dimensional theory had more equations than Einstein's four-dimensional version and the extra equations turned out to be Maxwell's equations governing the electromagnetic field. Not even

Einstein could figure out where the extra dimension was. Most of the subsequent research had it being a microscopic cylinder, or some other compact shape too small to see.

As far as modern science is concerned, the fifth dimension is purely hypothetical. A place we can never go, never see and from which we will never get any information. But the precise equations for the electromagnetic field didn't come out of Kaluza's theory by happenstance. The fifth dimension is real, and its existence can be demonstrated experimentally.

The fourth dimension of space is as big as the three we are aware of. It is part of our Universe and its right in front of us. The reason we don't see it is that our brains, since our ancestors crawled out of the ground after the dinosaurs were destroyed, evolved without seeing it. When our tools advanced enough to allow us to view the Universe on a grand scale we saw evidence of the fifth dimension in the form of the elongated frequency of light coming from distant galaxies. That evidence was misinterpreted as an expanding Universe and that error sent cosmologist down an incorrect path that the entire physics community has followed ever since.

An accurate, if not quite precise, way to envision the fourth spacial dimension is that it is at rest relative to our three-dimensional space. Three-dimensional space is moving relative to the fourth dimension at 186,000 miles per second, what we measure as the speed of light. The speed of light is actually zero.

The Sun is decelerating away from the Earth. We don't see it moving because we see, think and measure in three dimensions and it is moving in a direction of the fourth dimension. All gravity is deceleration. All powered movement is deceleration. When you approach a Black Hole, time slows because space slows. A very fast spaceship wouldn't accelerate to near the speed of light, it would decelerate to nearly a stop.

The speed of light is a fundamental limit because you can't slow beyond a stop. If you are traveling down the highway at a high speed, you can apply force to the brake and decrease your speed. The more force you apply, the faster you decelerate, until you come to a stop. After that you can apply all the force you want, but you have reached a fundamental limit. Time is a function of the velocity of space, so what you are actually doing is running out of time, but the analogy is accurate.

The attempt to stay on a path that leads in the wrong direction has led cosmologists to some bizarre conclusions. Dark Energy, a mysterious repulsive force no scientist has ever seen experimentally. They don't even have a good guess as to what it is, it's just a fudge factor to explain why the Universe we see doesn't conform to the accepted theory. Inflation in the early Universe is another fudge factor that serves no purpose beyond preserving a flawed theory.

The theory that the Universe is expanding has the embarrassing feature of having had to begin as a singularity in which the whole thing was compressed into an infinitely small spec. It makes more sense to assume, taking a page from conventional science, that energy is conserved. Energy didn't pop into existence out of nothing 14 billion years ago, it has always been there. It is the kinetic energy of a Universe moving at 186,000 miles per second.

We live in an evolving universe. Something happened 10 or so billion years ago, probably an interaction with something in the fourth dimension, which began the process of converting some of the kinetic energy in our neighborhood of space to matter, at the cost of some of the velocity of space. Using modern telescopes like Hubble, we can see other distant regions of space where the same thing occurred or is occurring. Existing Galaxies and the formation of new galaxies.

Gravity slows the observed passage of time and light frequency acts as a clock. Gravity is deceleration, so the distance between an observer in space and light from a decelerated source does increase in four-dimensional space without the need for space itself to expand. The frequency of light from distant galaxies is a five-dimensional phenomena that is easily observable by humans for the same reason the curvature of Earth is easier to discern from a greater distance.

When the satellite COBE was sent out to analyze Cosmic Background Radiation, it discovered a complex and detailed structure rather than the featureless glow predicted by Big Bang cosmologists. Rather than question the assumption that the signal was from the Big Bang, they did the same thing Copernicus did, figured out a way to make the data fit into the existing theory. It took a thousand years to give up epicycles.

The most distant object measured by the Hubble Telescope is 13 billion light years away, which means it would have had to have been created when the universe was less than one billion years old. It would take at least that long for the material from the Big Bang to coalesce into stars and form a young galaxy.

Recently a galaxy called SPT–S J041839–4751.9 was discovered using the South Pole Telescope. Follow-up observations made using the more powerful Atacama Large Millimeter/Submillimeter Array revealed a relatively normal disk-shaped galaxy like the Milky Way, although about a quarter the size of our galaxy. It has a flat disk of stars, gas, and dust, and even a central bulge of stars like the Milky Way.

It took the light from the object 12.4 billion years to reach Earth, so we are seeing that object as it was 12.4 billion years ago, where it was 12.4 billion years ago. All galaxies observed at that distance should appear very young, about one billion years old. It should not be a relatively mature spiral galaxy. It makes more sense to assume that it formed 12.4 billion light years from Earth by the same process that formed our galaxy.

A program at the California Institute of Technology called Galaxy Evolution Explorer has found three-dozen bright, compact galaxies that greatly resemble the youthful galaxies that would have existed more than 10 billion years ago in a Big Bang Universe. These are the galaxies we should be seeing at 13 billion light years distant, but these new galaxies are relatively close to us, ranging from two to four billion light-years away and appear to be as young as 100 million to one billion years old.

In an infinite five-dimensional universe, the process of converting kinetic energy to mass could continue in new regions of space forever. Any region of space that eventually converts all of its energy would have no velocity, come to a stop. That region would look like a Black Hole. The background radiation of this infinite space would be low energy, long wavelength light broken up by random areas of kinetic space and Black Holes. Much like the Cosmic Microwave Background we measure today.

Quantum Physics is the four-dimensional study of five-dimensional phenomena, which has led to some strange conclusions. It has been demonstrated many times with the double slit experiment, done with photons or electrons, it has even been done with molecules. The result is that each individual particle or molecule sent toward the slits one at a time, pass through both slits and create an interference pattern on a detector behind the slits.

Do the experiment a million times and you will get the same result every time, until you watch to see which slit the particle or molecule goes through. Do exactly the same experiment another million times while watching the slits, and each time the pattern on the detector shows a hit behind whichever slit you saw the thing go through. No interference pattern just because you possess knowledge that you didn't possess through the first million experiments.

When we look closely at fundamental particles, we see them interacting with five-dimensional space-time and interpret it as the wave function of matter. The exact position and momentum of an electron cannot be simultaneously determined because an electron is a four-dimensional point particle that defies measurement in three dimensions. The waviness in quantum physics is another glimpse of the fifth dimension. When we look too closely at a particle that behaved as a wave a million times, our minds collapse it into our three-dimensional approximation of the real world.

It is accepted science today that uncertainty, non-locality and the wave-function of matter are properties of nature. The building blocks of matter have no basis in reality until the act of conscious observation collapses their wave function. If reality is to exist independent of human observation, there must be a better explanation for the apparent wave function of matter. A fifth macro-dimension of space is a better explanation.

Hawking Radiation. On the face of it, if a pair of virtual particles appear near the event horizon of a Black Hole, one falls in, the other escapes, you would think that both the Universe and the Black Hole gain energy. But according to Hawking, and the first Law of Thermal Dynamics, in order to preserve total energy, the particle that fell in must have negative energy, making the Black Hole evaporate. It was the culmination of an attempt from the 1950's and 60's to get around the relativistic "collapse out of existence" of matter at the center of a Black Hole.

In our five-dimensional Universe, virtual particles are a manifestation of the kinetic energy of moving space. They are part of the natural mechanism for converting kinetic energy to mass and explain the homogeneous nature of the visible universe. When a pair of virtual particles appear near an event horizon, and one of them falls in, the Universe and the Black Hole gain energy offset by a local decrease in the speed of three-dimensional space. Quantum Physics and General Relativity get along fine.

The velocity of space creates time. Time makes space multi-dimensional. Matter is the energy of space manifested in multiple dimensions. When gravity becomes strong enough to slow a region of space to a stop, time ceases to exist in that region and space reverts to one dimension. The space beyond the event horizon is not three-dimensional space warped by a singularity, it is simple, one-dimensional space.

The phenomena surrounding an event horizon are explained by the fact that gravity acts against the velocity of 3-dimensional space. As space slows, time slows and multidimensional space warps toward one dimension. If you put a grape between the two plates of a giant tortilla press made out of neutrons and pressed them together until they touched, the grape would become two-dimensional. If you had a five-dimensional tortilla press and put pressure on a four-dimensional Earth, you would cause tides.

Photons. When mass has momentum, it can exert force by spending velocity without losing mass energy (except a bit of heat from an impact). Momentum is energy borrowed from acceleration. In five-dimensional relativity, acceleration is deceleration. Photons are massless particles that carry energy via its momentum relative to three-dimensional space, the energy belongs to space. Every time science shows us something in the fifth dimension, we assume it disappeared. When the frequency of light from a star that collapses into a black hole decreases to a straight line, it doesn't cease to exist, it ceases to interact with moving three-dimensional space.

According to General Relativity, super massive objects have gravity fields so strong that not even light can escape. Since the entire universe existing in just one spot would be the most massive object of all, the universe could not have escaped in a Big Bang. Every science class, every college science course, every science documentary on the Discovery channel, the entirety of establishment science claims that it did.

To explain the discrepancy, the entirety of the physics community agree that the laws of physics just didn't apply at the time of the Big Bang. They agree that the known universe spans 28 billion light years and is assumed to be 14 billion years old. For that to be true, we would need to be at the center of the universe because otherwise it would extend even further in at least one direction making it older than 14 billion years.

The theory that the universe is expanding uniformly would mean that the amount of red shifts would have to be uniformly and randomly distributed. They aren't. The observed red shifts are quantized, falling into discreet intervals. This is not explainable by the theory that the Universe is expanding. Some other effect is at work unless they have another "laws of physics don't apply here" solution.

The assumption that there must be a beginning to the universe is an invention of the human mind. We think we see things begin and end, but we are really just seeing matter change form. A particular configuration may have a beginning and an end, but the actual matter and energy cannot be created or destroyed, it has always been. Until recently, "scientists" believed that the Earth was the center of the universe. Now they claim that the edge of the Universe is 14 billion light years distant in every direction from Earth. The contention that everything was at the center in the beginning and that everything is moving away from everything else doesn't really get the Earth out of the center.

We see objects out to the edge of the limits of our technology and we see them in all directions. We can't see an edge of the universe, but the scientific consensus is that it's there, beyond what we can see. It makes more sense to assume that what we can see is really just a small part of a far larger universe. If we abandon the assumption that we see most of the universe from a fortunate position near the location of the original singularity, then we cannot know how large the universe is, and the mathematics by which we claim to know the age of the Universe based on its size is flawed.

Even if the Universe ends just beyond the limits of our technological ability to measure, it is still too big for the Big Bang theory. The original singularity would have an event horizon many light years larger than the size of the Universe when the current theory says inflation ended and all the fundamental forces came into play. It could not have escaped.

The physics communities answer? You guessed it, "the laws of physics don't apply here". They developed the theory that when the universe was created, it had no mass, so there was no gravity and no reason the Big Bang matter couldn't escape into the universe. Then, after it was far enough away from the singularity, it interacted with a particle called a Higgs Boson, also called the God particle because they needed a miracle to save their Big Bang creation theory.

Five billion dollars later, they managed to kinda, sorta create a Higgs Boson in the Large Hadron Collider. Once again, they found what they wanted to find, the Big Bang theory is safe, and I can't possibly know what I'm talking about because I don't have an advanced degree.

The No Big Bang Theory, or Five-Dimensional Relativity, is consistent with the contemporary body of experimental data without needing to suspend fundamental forces to make it work. The Big Bang Theory is not.

Aliens, Ancient or Otherwise

If the current understanding of Quantum Mechanics is an accurate description of the world, there are no aliens. The building blocks of matter have no basis in reality until the act of conscious observation collapses their wave function. The stars didn't exist as other suns until we discovered them. The Universe was only as large as we could see with our naked eyes until our imagination and Galileo's telescope made it larger.

Thankfully Quantum Mechanics, as currently espoused by physicists is wrong. The Universe is unimaginably large, and it exists whether we are conscious of it or not. There are countless alien individuals, colonies and civilizations scattered across the Universe. We're not likely to see any of them because they are spread out so far in space and time that the odds of any two of them meeting are literally astronomical. The odds of one of them being Earthlings are even greater.

The wonder of life on Earth is that millions of criteria had to be exactly as they are, where they are, when they are and arranged just as they are, for life to exist. That would be exceedingly unlikely in a 14-billion-year-old Universe that was only 28 billion light years across. In a very much larger Universe, it would be more likely. In an infinite Universe, it would be inevitable. Since we are here, the Universe must be very large, likely infinite, which would make not just the conventional understanding of Quantum Mechanics wrong, the Big Bang theory of the origin of the Universe and the claim that the Universe is expanding are also wrong.

What about UFOs? The military has admitted they have no idea what they are. "Their actions defy the laws of physics as we know them." That should be a clue. The first time someone said something like that they were talking about bumble bees. Which don't defy the laws of physics, but they appear to at first glance. Our understanding of the life forms we share this planet with is tainted by ignorance born of arrogance.

Human civilization was shaped by the fact that we have hands, but civilization did not happen because we had hands, it happened because we have brains. If a species had a brain comparable to ours, but no hands, their civilization would look much different. We probably wouldn't even recognize it as a civilization. Before we look for alien intelligence that lives thousands or millions of times more distant than the size, we think the Universe is, we should look for it among the millions of species on our own planet.

There is that book, movie and now TV series that shows sites around the world that purportedly prove that aliens visited Earth in the past. All those sites prove is that humans have built and lost civilizations many times throughout their history. The one we are in the process of destroying will leave fewer lasting artifacts than most.

The Moon Landing

The moon landing in 1969 was one of the greatest achievements of the human species, and it was a demonstration of the superiority of the American system. Planting the American flag on the moon surpassed the liberation of Europe after WWII as a symbol of human potential and hope for the future.

It is easy to believe that the U.S. government was responsible, NASA was a government agency after all, but that's wrong. The people responsible for humans going to the Moon were the Wright Brothers, Ford, Carnegie, Rockefeller, Tesla and thousands more who took advantage of being free to invent, innovate, create, build, make money, and incidentally advance the human race.

When the government got involved, it looked like progress and sounded aspirational, but fifty years later it was easy to see that it was the vinegar that curdled process. The government took the progress and the wealth that the American people created during a hundred years of freedom and used it to win a war and go to the Moon, and then they kept it, because once the government gets something (never let a crisis go to waste) they never give it up. We made that giant leap, and then nothing. For over fifty years since going to the Moon, the government spent an amount exceeding all the spending for the previous history of the nation and accomplished nothing. It has failed to keep every promise.

The United States has been under siege by the global ruling class whose priorities are incompatible with individual freedom. They have fostered a movement that believes it is unfair for the United States to be so successful while most of the world is poor, and who are uncomfortable with the United States planting our flag on the Moon. That might be part of the reason we have shunned the Moon for fifty years, but there is more to it.

It is possible that one of the reasons is rooted in how the Moon was created in the first place. The generally accepted hypothesis is that the Moon formed out of debris left over from a collision between Earth and an astronomical body the size of Mars approximately 4.5 billion years ago. As the Earth cooled, its gravity concentrated heavier elements toward the center of the planet, leaving those elements rare near the crust. The astronomical object plowed through the Earth's core and created a debris field that eventually coalesced into the Moon. A Moon that was neither molten nor large enough to have the gravity that gave Earth its mostly iron core, so the Moon is made of the same materials as Earth, but its heavy metals are not concentrated in its core.

In July of 1969, man first stepped foot on the Moon. In August of 1971, Nixon took the U.S. dollar off the gold standard. For the next fifty years, the United States went out of its way to keep the worlds manned space aspirations in Earth orbit. That policy has run its course. In 2009, NASA put a reconnaissance satellite in orbit around the Moon, ostensibly to map its surface, but its main purpose was to conduct a geological survey and to monitor activity on the Moon of which there will soon be quite a lot.

India, China, the European Space Agency and at least two private companies have all started or will soon start mining operations on the Moon. They mostly claim to be looking for a theoretical nuclear fuel called Helium 3, but I think their true motivation might provide a more dependable return on their investment. They need, for propaganda purposes if nothing else, the basis for a world currency. Finding it on the Moon will fit into their global narrative quite nicely.

We should have returned to the Moon, gone to Mars, the moons of Saturn and beyond. The reason we didn't is greed. Small, short-sighted politicians who when given the reins of a once in a civilization, maybe once in a species political system with the means to fulfill human destiny, chose to enrich themselves instead.

Most of the trillions our government spends every year are on things that are blatantly outside its constitutional purview, it is illegal. In fact, the federal government has evolved into little more than the world's largest embezzlement scheme hidden behind a facade of representative government.

Pyramids of Egypt

Who built the Pyramids? We may never know. I can tell you that what you were taught in school, that they were built by a primitive, pre-technological society, is not true.

After several thousand years of various "experts and scientists" trying to explain Khufu's pyramid, there is still no agreement on how many stones it took, let alone how a people who had yet to invent the wheel or pulley managed to quarry 2.5 million "estimates range from 600,000 to 7,000,000" stones weighing 2 to 70 tons, move them 500 miles and fit them together into a structure that covers 13 acres and towers 481 feet. If we built it today using modern technology, the Great Pyramid would cost more than the entire space program from Alan Shepard in 1961 to the Mars lander, and it would take longer.

It is widely accepted that the Great Pyramid was built over a twenty-year period during the reign of the Pharaoh Khufu (2589-2566 BC), based on some marks found in a chamber that references Khufu, marks that could have been placed there long after the pyramid's construction. All of the evidence used to date the pyramid to Khufu's time, tombs, pottery, hieroglyphics, are actually evidence that the Egyptians of Khufu's time, found the pyramids. There are no hieroglyphics in or on the pyramids, only on the things people who lived around them made. That, along with the fact that the society that lived around the pyramids during Khufu's time did not possess the technology to have constructed them, make it obvious that the pyramids were built by a society that necessarily did possess the technology to have constructed them, long before Khufu's time.

There are hint's gleaned from ancient writings of a technology that allowed people to levitate heavy objects using sound, or something that made a sound. Here is an experiment I first saw in grade school that demonstrates how the technology could have worked. Tear a piece of toilet paper into small pieces and put them in a lose pile on the table. Then run a plastic comb back and forth through your hair. Now wave the comb over the paper. The paper will float back and forth following the comb. Some of them will even float up and stick to the comb. The static electricity is a buildup of electrons in the comb. When you wave it over the paper, the negative charge in the comb repels the electrons in the paper's atoms giving the side of them facing the comb a positive charge, or more accurately, a less negative charge. Technology that could polarize the electrons in a block of stone, and in a section of the Earth's crust, would make building large stone structures easy. You would only be limited by how high you could stack them before gravity crushed the base. This limitation would steer larger structures towards a pyramid shape.

Today's experts are limited by the erroneous belief that the 4 or 5 generations leading up to their own, are the only ones out of the 4,000 that came before to develop any kind of technology.

Epilogue

We can say what we please on social media and national media only if it conforms to ruling class guidelines. We are allowed only the portion of our wages the ruling class sees fit to leave for us. We can step foot on public property only with permission. We can operate our private vehicle on public roads if it was manufactured by an approved company, if it is powered by an approved fuel and we haven't tampered with any of its emission, safety or surveillance features. We can stay in our "paid for" homes on our "paid for" land as long as we pay the government each year for the privilege. It's time to admit that we are not free and haven't been for a long time.

If Donald Trump is allowed to remain free and to live long enough, he will run for President in 2024. If an election can be fairly conducted, which is very unlikely, he could wrest this country from the ruling class who stole it in 1913. If he does, and if he successfully returns power to the people, he will go down in history as a traitor because it will piss off some enormously powerful people and they control every channel that is piped into our homes every day.

Since I learned how to read in 1968 or so, I have read continuously. If I couldn't find a good book, I would read whatever I could get my hands on. This will sound strange today, but I was given a bible in grade school. I read it, cover to cover. What my eleven-year-old mostly science fiction reading mind took from it, without the benefit of organized religion, was that it was a story, distorted by time, of a species destined to explore the Universe and live forever. The story of an ancient civilization that had discovered the secret to immortality, but were thwarted by greed, envy and dishonesty. I had seen Neil Armstrong step onto the Moon, and I was sure that by the time I was an adult, Mars and a cure for old age would be within reach.

The U.S. Constitution was usurped in 1913 and the greedy lying bastards who took control, spent the next hundred plus years trading our destiny for mere money. They still run the world. Somewhere in the neighborhood of 16 thousand years have passed since the last iteration of human civilization left its legacy in a layer of fused green glass. Surely the Universe will give us another sixteen thousand years to try again.

References

Most of the information in this book was derived directly from the use of Common Sense. I also gleaned information from thousands of books read continuously, often two at a time, since sometime in 1969. Other information was derived from the following.

The Immaculate Deception: Six Key Dimensions of Election Irregularities. By Peter Navarro

Federation of American Scientists: Project on Government Secrecy

The following U.S. government sources were relied on for statistical information.

U.S. Declassified Documents Online

Digital National Security Archive External Restricted Access

CIA: Electronic Reading Room

Department of State: Freedom of Information Act

FBI Records: The Vault - FOIA Library

In the few instances when information in this book was found on Google, Google is referenced in the sentence in which the information appears.

Neither Facebook nor Twitter were used in any part of this book. All references to Facebook or Twitter were taken from news reports and used sparingly.

Dan Fragoules is a businessman, pilot and author. He is married, has two adult sons and lives on eighty or so secluded acres in the Ozark mountains.